# 40 Conversations:
## A Guided Journal for Personal and Professional Growth

This journal belongs to: _____

This journey began on: _____

My encouraging mentor (if applicable) was: _____

I completed the journey on: _____

My favorite conversations were:

_____

_____

_____

_____

Notes to revisit, or key points to remember:

_____

_____

_____

_____

_____

# 40 Conversations:
## A Guided Journal for Personal and Professional Growth

Clarify your purpose. Advance your career. Create the future you want.

Brian Raison, PhD

Featuring prompts from *The Encouraging Mentor: Your Guide to 40 Conversations that Matter*

WESTBOW
PRESS®
A DIVISION OF THOMAS NELSON
& ZONDERVAN

Copyright © 2024 Brian Raison.

All rights reserved. No part of this book may be used or reproduced by any means, graphic, electronic, or mechanical, including photocopying, recording, taping or by any information storage retrieval system without the written permission of the author except in the case of brief quotations embodied in critical articles and reviews.

This book is a work of non-fiction. Unless otherwise noted, the author and the publisher make no explicit guarantees as to the accuracy of the information contained in this book and in some cases, names of people and places have been altered to protect their privacy.

WestBow Press books may be ordered through booksellers or by contacting:

WestBow Press
A Division of Thomas Nelson & Zondervan
1663 Liberty Drive
Bloomington, IN 47403
www.westbowpress.com
844-714-3454

Because of the dynamic nature of the Internet, any web addresses or links contained in this book may have changed since publication and may no longer be valid. The views expressed in this work are solely those of the author and do not necessarily reflect the views of the publisher, and the publisher hereby disclaims any responsibility for them.

Any people depicted in stock imagery provided by Getty Images are models, and such images are being used for illustrative purposes only. Certain stock imagery © Getty Images.

Author Photo by John Noltner

ISBN: 979-8-3850-1259-6 (sc)
ISBN: 979-8-3850-1260-2 (e)

Print information available on the last page.

WestBow Press rev. date: 01/19/2024

# Contents

**Beginning Your Journey:**

**Setting the Context** ................................................................. 3

**How to Use This Journal** ........................................................ 6

**The Conversations:**

**Initiating Growth**

    1. Who Are You? (The Launch Conversation) .................... 11
    2. The Being-Remembered Conversation ........................ 14
    3. Five Things to Have, Do, Help, and Be: *A Personal Futuring Exercise* .......................................................... 16
    4. The Bucket List ............................................................. 19
    5. The Values Review ....................................................... 23
    6. Your Personal Mission .................................................. 25
    7. Leveraging Gratitude .................................................... 29
    8. Building Curiosity ........................................................ 32

**Deepening Connections**

    9. From Why? to What? .................................................... 37
   10. Feeling Safe .................................................................. 41

11. What's Your Biggest Fear? *A Check-in for Mental Health* .......... 44
12. Bravery. Failure. Kindness. .................................................. 48
13. Joy vs. Happiness: *Finding Fulfillment in Work and Life* ........... 51
14. Remembering to Listen *(to Others and Yourself)* ..................... 54

## Career Advancement

15. Who You Are *vs.* What You Do .............................................. 61
16. What Motivates You? ........................................................... 63
17. Change. Growth Mindset. Ambiguity. Three Skills for Career Advancement .................................................................. 66
18. Reframing Six Stages of a Career *(from Ladder to Scaffold)* ..... 69
19. Handling Critics and Criticism: *A Growth Mindset Approach* ................................................... 73
20. Providing Clarity ................................................................. 76
21. Triangulating Your Skills, Abilities, and Interests to Find Your Future ................................................................. 79
22. The Resume & Cover Letter: *Always be Prepared* .................... 82
23. Real Interview Tips that Work ................................................ 85
24. The Stay Interview: *Is Staying an Opportunity?* ...................... 89
25. Financial Health: Two Keys for Success (Live and Give) .......... 93
    a. Live ................................................................................ 93
    b. Give ............................................................................... 96

## Expanding Points of View

26. E+R=O (Event + Response = Outcome) ............................... 101
27. Circle of Control: *Shift Your Focus. Reduce Worry.* ............... 104
28. Hidden Diversity ................................................................ 107
29. Seek Diverse Relationships .................................................. 110
30. Building Your Emotional Intelligence (EQ) .......................... 113
31. Building Your Social Intelligence ......................................... 117

32. Generation C: Connectivity ................................................... 120
33. Spirituality & Faith Traditions ............................................ 123
34. Changing Perspective: *Embracing the Art of Possibility* ........... 127

**Anytime Conversation Prompts**

35. Perspective Shifting ............................................................ 133
36. The Charles Schulz Challenge: Embracing Contentment ...... 137
37. Building Trust ..................................................................... 141
38. The Power of Vision: An Indispensable Skill ..................... 145
39. Storytelling: A Useful Tool in Any Career ......................... 148
40. Leading with Humility ........................................................ 152

**20 Bonus Questions to Encourage Continued Thinking** ............... 157

**In summary** ........................................................................................ 167

**About the Author** ............................................................................. 173

# Beginning Your Journey

# Setting the Context

> The greatest scarcity you will face in your professional life is not a scarcity of opportunity, but a scarcity of meaning.
> - James Choi

Imagine a point in the future where you have achieved your greatest professional goal. Invest a moment here. Try to visualize your career success—you at the top of your game. Imagine you've worked hard and have earned it. Now consider this question: *How might that success feel?*

I think most people will have some level of contentment or satisfaction. Others may feel a bit of pride in the accomplishment. Some may begin to ponder, "What's next?" Those responses are all normal and valid. But now, imagine it's *one month after* that major achievement. Consider these questions:

- How do you feel now (one month later)?
- What is motivating you now (since you've accomplished your greatest career goal)?
- What occupies your time and your thinking now (both at work and at home)?

Yale professor and economist James Choi tells his students that the greatest scarcity they will face in their professional lives is not a scarcity of opportunity, but a scarcity of *meaning*. He contends that finding happiness in life can be accomplished only by knowing our *why*.

Choi explains that thinking about some future ultimate success or reaching major life goals can become *arrival fallacies*. Here, we mistakenly believe that we achieve happiness only after achieving a particular goal. This, he contends, can lead to deep disappointment.

This was my story. It has taken me years to understand, but looking back, I can see why I felt no real joy when I achieved some fairly high goals early in my career. I certainly experienced happiness in those moments, but there was always something missing, and I did not know what it was.

Early in my professional career, I was at the right place at the right time on numerous occasions. Because of my upbringing, I worked hard. But I attributed everything to *luck*. From international travel to job offers, I found more success than I ever dreamed. I had the obligatory red sports car and the best camping equipment. I also had a huge *disconnect* with feeling satisfied. I had no idea what was missing or why I felt such a void.

So I quit. And I sold the car. To the dismay of my parents, I left my Fortune 500 job and told everyone I was going camping for a month. Several months later (and still camping), my brother called and said he needed help with a volunteer project. There were three hundred high school and college students coming to town to do home repairs for low-resource community members—and I happened to have basic skills as a painter, roofer, plumber, electrician, and so forth. The work was being done through a faith-based organization out of Colorado who engaged people "to make a difference for others." It was a simple idea that helped a community, but often had profound impact on the volunteers. I was one of them.

After that week, I discovered that serving others brings me joy. This will not be the case for everyone, of course. But for me, I had discovered something new. I have subsequently read research studies that show how service to others is, arguably, one of the most impactful things anyone can do to increase satisfaction and joy in their life. Though I'd volunteered before, this experience was somehow different. Again, I got lucky and somehow arrived at the right place at the right time.

Unfortunately, I was not independently wealthy. Being single with no dependents and debt-free had allowed me to stretch my savings for nearly a year. But I knew it was time to go back to work. Because of my volunteer discoveries, I wanted to find work that was *meaningful*. In early 1996, I applied for a job with Ohio State University Extension that spoke to my new-found *why*. It was half the salary I'd previously enjoyed, and they almost did not hire me because of that. Luckily, I convinced them I was looking for something fulfilling. They gave me a chance. I quickly realized I'd found something for my professional life that had *purpose* and resonated with my newfound focus.

Let's return to our Yale professor, Dr. Choi. He maintains that the only way to find contentment and happiness in life is to identify *a purpose*. Our purpose answers *why* we get up in the morning and go to work. It answers *why* we live, *why* we laugh, and *why* we love. It answers the deepest existential questions of our *raison d'etre*. Please note, if you have not yet formally articulated your *purpose* or *mission* in life, this journal will guide you through that in Conversation 6. I was around thirty-five when I first outlined my personal mission. It's never too early or late. You can begin at any age.

As you move through all forty of these reflective conversations, you will be challenged to dig below the surface to consider what really matters in life. There are likely several questions herein that you have never been asked. These will lead you to think about your real purpose and see beyond surface-level professional achievement.

Now, here's the cool part. As the questions help you zero-in on meaning and purpose, you will, subsequently, become more valuable in the workplace. Walking through this process of deep, missional thinking will provide clarity. It will give you the courage to leave a job you dislike, or stay and improve one that has potential. This inward focus will help your outward leadership skillset grow.

From the earliest ages, my daughters heard me proclaim, sometimes with a bad fake British accent, "I care not what you do in life, career-wise, or what your income may be. I want only for you to have joy in the journey." They—along with my students, coworkers, and my continuing desire for personal growth—provided a collective reason for me to put together these forty mentoring conversation tools over the years. Thinking through deep questions can help us find *internal* fulfillment—not simply career success.

Our personal and professional selves are intertwined, even if we try to hold them apart. This journal—*this journey*—will help you see how everything can come together with purpose and meaning.

Are you ready for the challenge? Are you ready for the opportunity? Are you ready to define and live your purpose? The time to begin is now.

## How to Use This Journal

Reflection and journaling are proven methods that help us retain things we learn. They also help us think about our thinking, the very definition of metacognition. These are powerful tools.

This guided journal is a companion workbook that uses questions from *The Encouraging Mentor: Your Guide to 40 Conversations that Matter*. It provides a place for you to write reflections while talking with a mentor, or you may simply use this journal as an *independent study exercise* for personal and professional growth. Either way, it will help.

Each of the forty entries herein includes a brief introduction that provides background and context. It uses questions to prompt your thinking on topics that include life purpose and mission, career advancement, expanding your perspective, increasing connectivity, and identifying your potential to create and achieve the future you want. This journal will help you identify leadership skills, strengths, and opportunities that you might not *yet* see in yourself.

As you are moving through the journal, you might encounter times when you hear yourself saying, "I just can't do this. I don't see how I can improve." This is normal. Everyone has negative thoughts at times. But here's the reality: just because you *think* something does not mean it's true. Though we usually cannot control our negative thoughts, we can take steps to limit their volume (or at least redirect).

How do you change the conversation in your head? This may sound overly simple, but whenever a negative thought creeps into your head, pretend *someone else* is saying it to you. Then, immediately tell them to stop. Seriously. Yell at them. *"Stop!"* Tell your mind you're not going to listen to things that aren't true, or if you tend to worry (as I do at times), tell yourself, "I am not going listen to things that may never happen." Then replace that negative voice with something good.

Here are two ideas on how to redirect negative thoughts:

1. Pull out your gratitude list. Read things you're grateful for aloud. Gratitude chases worry and negativity out the door. They cannot occupy the same space.
2. Write down your skill sets. Get out a piece of paper or send a text to yourself (right then in the moment). List things you have accomplished. List positive things in your life.

I have used both strategies. They have not always solved my issue, but they've helped me get through the moment.

If your self-talk should happen to bring up past problems, something bad that happened, or poor decisions (which we *all* have made at times), there's one additional strategy that can help. Say this aloud. Better yet, write it on a piece of paper.

"I will not let my past determine my future. Whether it was something bad that happened to me, or a poor decision I made, ***I will not let my past determine my future.***"

These are powerful words. These are words mentors have encouraged me to say in the past. This strategy will not make everything automatically better. But it can help. Remember, always seek professional counseling when needed. I'm a big proponent of that. But sometimes a counselor is not available in the moment. Or perhaps you have never set up an appointment like that before. That's okay. This exercise is a start. From here, you can continue your journey.

I wish you *good luck* as you learn and grow. Remember, luck is found at the intersection of preparation and opportunity. You're doing the preparation now. The opportunities await.

One last note: Along with unique questions for each topic, you will also have space to write general reflections on each topic. Writing helps cement learning. Please return to your notes over time to remember and to find inspiration. The summary questions in each conversation will help. They include: *1.) One thing that struck me about this topic was… 2.) I'm still pondering (and may seek more information on)… 3.) As a result of this reflection, I plan to…*

Please don't skip over these. They are important to the process. They can help you understand that just because you don't have some specific skill *yet*, you are still on the path moving forward. *Yet* is the operative word as you move forward.

Are you ready? Let's begin with Conversation 1.

# Conversations for Initiating Growth

# Conversation 1

## Who Are You? (The Launch Conversation)

**Background:** As noted, this journal extracted question prompts from a companion book, *The Encouraging Mentor*. If you are completing this journal with a mentor, your entries will reflect talking with another person. But if you are using this resource on your own for personal and professional development, you can *still* ask yourself these questions. (I modified some of them slightly, so they make sense either way.) In completing this journal, you are engaging in self-reflection and metacognition—thinking about how you think. These are invaluable exercises. Let's begin.

**Question 1**

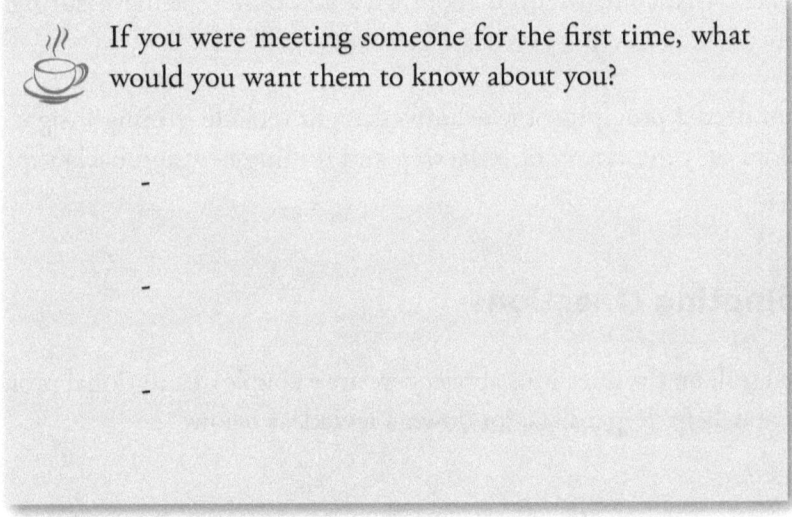

Once you have thought about the basics, take the time to follow trails of your interests. *Be curious.* Let me repeat that one: *On your own or with a mentor, be curious.* Ask yourself why you wrote some of the items above. Then proceed to the next question.

## Question 2

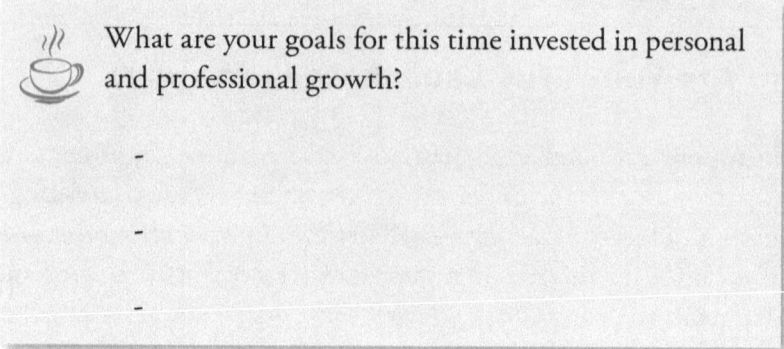

What are your goals for this time invested in personal and professional growth?

On the surface, the question above sounds heavy duty, but don't let it weigh down your thinking too much. The idea for today is to just get started. Goals will shift and change over time. That's okay, and it is a natural occurrence. So no worries there. For today, simply name one or two ideas that come to mind about what you want to achieve during this journey.

If you need a prompt, some examples might include gaining insight and wisdom on your career, or reflecting and finding new approaches for life issues.

## Prompting Questions

If you stall on the questions above, here are a couple of additional prompts that may help. Regardless, jot down a few ideas below.

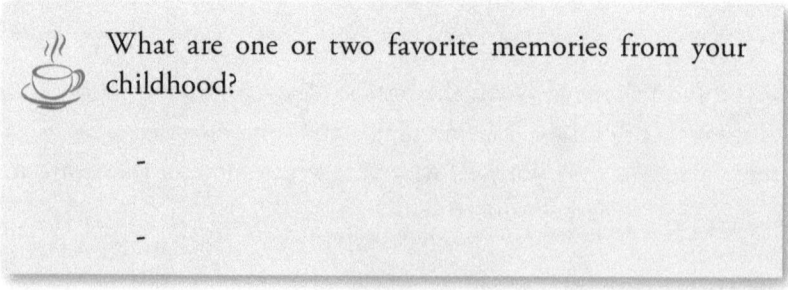

What are one or two favorite memories from your childhood?

The question above is reflective. By using the qualifier "favorite," it aims to start an appreciative inquiry in your brain. Imagine how you might let favorite memories help direct a positive path forward. That idea might be furthered by considering the next question.

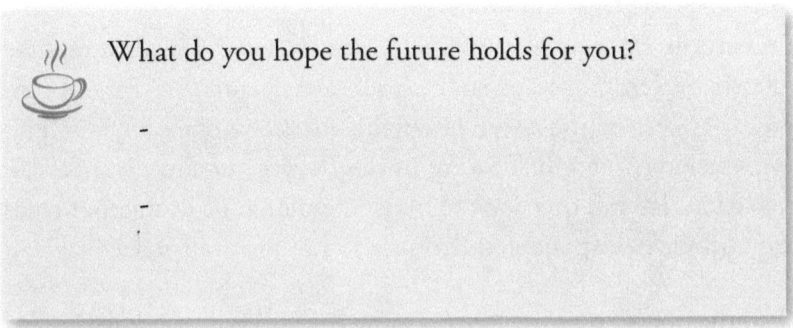

What do you hope the future holds for you?

The question above is broad by design at this early stage. After jotting a few ideas, consider what else you'd share if a mentor said, "Tell me more."

**Summary:** Remember these introductory prompts are to jump-start your thinking about the foundations of your life *so far*. From here, you will begin diving into questions that will challenge you to go deeper, considering possibility and potential. Investing time to reflect starts you on a path that will help you clarify your purpose, advance your career, and identify potential to create the future you want.

## General Reflections:

One thing that struck me about this topic was: _____
_____

I'm still pondering *(and may seek more information on)*: _____
_____

As a result of this reflection, I plan to: _____
_____
_____

# Conversation 2

## The Being-Remembered Conversation

**Background:** *How do you want to be remembered?* This is a rephrase of the classic Steven Covey question from *The 7 Habits of Highly Effective People*. It is one of the most powerful questions one can ever ponder. (Note: Versions of it will show up in the *Bucket List* and *Personal Mission* conversations later in this book. This is intentional.) Throughout recorded history, people have pondered the question of life's purpose.

Look at the question below. Spend some time with it. It is a definite brain engager because we are often too busy to pause and reflect in this way. So for most, the question will linger for a while.

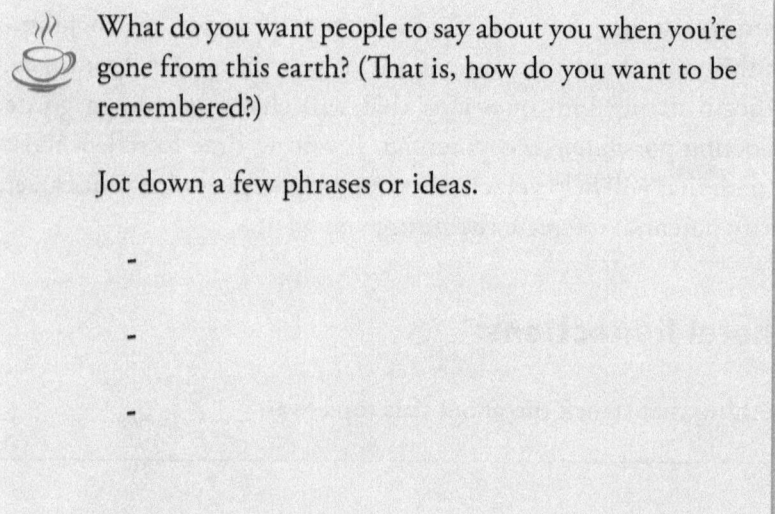

What do you want people to say about you when you're gone from this earth? (That is, how do you want to be remembered?)

Jot down a few phrases or ideas.

- 
- 
- 

Let these ideas ruminate a bit. If able, go outside or take a walk or roll. Be curious about what you've written. Consider questions that might come to mind, including, *"What else?"* You may even let your responses sit for a week. But then, go deeper. Think about how to boil it down to the basics:

> Look at your responses above. Are there some items you could group together or summarize? Jot down a few summary ideas.
>
> - 
>
> - 
>
> - 
>
> Challenge:
>
> Can you boil this down to one or two words?

**Homework:** Return to this after completing Conversation 6, the *Personal Mission* challenge. Compare your responses. Chat with a mentor or good friend about this reflection.

**Bonus challenge:** *Pose the first question to them!*

## General Reflections:

One thing that struck me about this topic was: _____
_____

I'm still pondering *(and may seek more information on)*: _____
_____

As a result of this reflection, I plan to: _____
_____
_____

## Conversation 3

### Five Things to Have, Do, Help, and Be:
*A Personal Futuring Exercise*

**Background:** Everyone—every company, every non-profit, etc.—has two options for the future. There is the one that *will* be if we do nothing (continue the status quo) or the one that *could* be if we work to achieve it (plan and act to reach desired ends, goals, dreams, mission). Peter Drucker said it best: "The best way to predict the future is to create it."

At a very early age, most people are asked, "What do you want to be when you grow up?" We often prompt young minds with examples: "Do you want to be a firefighter? A teacher? A farmer?"

But what if there is a more important question: "Who do you want to become?" This is qualitatively different. This is perhaps the best question to ask to prompt future thinking, focus, and goal setting.

Read over the chart below. Then fill in each box with some ideas.

*What are five things you want...*

| ...to have: (These can be tangible or intangible.) | ...to do: (This is about *what* you might do: jobs, careers, things for fun, bucket list items, etc.) |
|---|---|
|  |  |

| ...to help: (These can be big and small. Think broadly.) | ...to be: (Not *what* you might do, but *who* you might become.) |
|---|---|
| | |

**Analysis:** Look at your responses. Will the things you want to do move you in the direction of things you want to have and to help? If not, add some actions to the to-do list, then prioritize. But remember, you cannot do everything. A prioritization strategy is to put some broad target dates next to your to-do items (e.g., within five years).

**Challenge:** The "to be" category will reflect how people remember you, now or when you're gone. Consider two action items that will help you accomplish *who* you want to be and *how* you want to be remembered. These may be short or long-term actions. Jot these down.

1.

2.

**Homework:** Carry this around, think, reflect, and update it over the next few weeks. You might discuss insights with your mentor, a trusted friend, or a family member.

## General Reflections:

One thing that struck me about this topic was: _____
_____

I'm still pondering *(and may seek more information on)*: _____
_____

As a result of this reflection, I plan to: _____
_____
_____

**Conversation 4**

## The Bucket List

**Purpose:** To help you continue and deepen your thinking about what matters most in life.

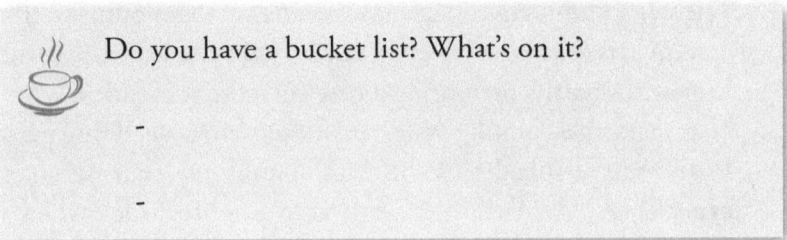

Do you have a bucket list? What's on it?

Most of us have some things we'd like to do or accomplish in life. Some of us write a formal list on paper. Others have lists in their heads. Often, the bucket list resides in our personal lives, but having one in our professional lives can make us more effective leaders as well.

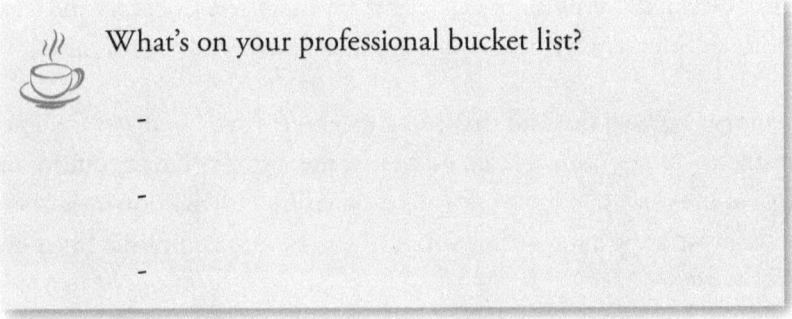

What's on your professional bucket list?

**The Detail:** Do you realize that—by definition and logic—If you have a bucket list, you're thinking about dying? That may seem morbid, but it is in fact a good thing to think about what you want to do before you die. In their 2016 publication *The Book of Joy*, the Dalai Lama and Bishop Desmond Tutu instruct us to consider our own mortality. They rightly contend that this will bring a sense of urgency, perspective, and gratitude. Author and pastor Andy Stanley similarly tells us that "priority determines capacity." He points to an ancient Jewish text (Psalm 90) that says, "teach us to number our days" in order to achieve wisdom. Numbering your days is thinking about how long you have to live, just as the bucket list has us thinking about specific things that we want to do while we're still alive. This can be powerful in helping us focus attention both at home and work.

Stanley also challenges us to "compound our minutes" noting (paraphrased):

1. There is a cumulative value to investing small amounts of time in certain activities over an extended period (e.g., exercise, spending time with family, mentoring a new coworker or student).
2. Neglect is also cumulative (e.g., *not* exercising, *not* doing personal finances, *not* spending time with family, *not* sharing your life experiences, *not* fulfilling leadership opportunities when they arise).
3. There is no cumulative value to the random things we opt for over the important things (e.g., surfing the internet, micromanaging instead of delegating).

If we're attentive to the limited time we have, we can use it more effectively. In turn, we can accomplish things that really matter. As mentors and leaders, we must simultaneously model this approach and behavior for others.

**Summary:** So how does all this come together? If you want to accomplish more and increase your capacity, make a bucket list. Try having one for home (personal life) and one for work (professional life). Write down those items that are most important—ones you really want to accomplish. Then begin.

What are one or two items from your bucket lists that you could begin to tackle in the next couple of days or weeks?

– Personal Bucket List:

– Professional Bucket List:

How might that help your _____ (career, personal life, studies, family, etc.)? (Choose one aspect and jot a few notes below.)

## For additional reference / reading:

Dalai Lama XIV, Desmond Tutu, and Douglas Carlton Abrams. *The Book of Joy: Lasting Happiness in a Changing World*. New York: Avery, 2016.

Stanley, Andy (Nov. 15, 2014). *Time Of Your Life 2 - At Capacity*. Available at: https://youtu.be/mIsnLZqmk_4

Stanley, Andy (Nov. 15, 2014). *Time Of Your Life 3 - Compounding Minutes*. Available at: https://youtu.be/YomJ6TUXChM

## General Reflections:

One thing that struck me about this topic was: _____
_____

I'm still pondering *(and may seek more information on)*: _____
_____

As a result of this reflection, I plan to: _____
_____
_____

# Conversation 5

## The Values Review

**Introduction:** As individuals, we all have varying values and belief systems. We come from differing backgrounds and places. This gives us a rich and beautiful diversity. But how do we incorporate values into our everyday work? How do we ensure our core values are the fundamental beliefs that guide behavior and action? Here's an exercise that will help.

**Instructions:**

1. In the table below, put a checkmark by items that you feel are important to you. Check as many as you want.

| Career | Respect | Cooperation | Popularity |
|---|---|---|---|
| Happiness | Freedom | Honesty | Fitting in |
| Service | Justice | Friendship | Pride |
| Courage | Fairness | Self-discipline | Loyalty |
| Love | Generosity | Responsibility | Community |
| Diversity | Compassion | Sharing | Progress |
| Perseverance | Beauty | Individuality | Spiritual / Faith |
| Reason | Patience | Prosperity | Wealth |
| Ambition | Creativity | Education | Family |
| Intelligence | Play | Belief | Tradition |
| Inclusion | Kindness | _____ | _____ |

2. Narrow the checked items to your top 10. <u>Underline</u> but do not rank.
3. Now, narrow to your top 5. Circle these.
4. Lastly, rank the circled items in order from 1 (most important) to 5 (less important).

**Questions to consider about your values:** *(Jot a few ideas for each.)*

1. Why do we need to know, name, and talk about our core values?

2. Who or what influenced your top values? (Consider family, society, geography, events.)

3. Have your top values changed over your lifetime? Will they? What might cause that?

**Questions to consider about other people and their values:** *(Jot a few ideas for each.)*

1. What happens when you need to work with someone whose values differ from yours?

2. Have you ever suppressed or temporarily ignored your values to fit in? (Or get a job? Etc.)

3. Can you respect someone who holds a fundamentally opposite value from you? How might you do that?

**Homework:** Look around for something that represents what is important to you. Perhaps it is something in nature, a quote, a sign, a person, or a pattern or design. Reflect on how that represents one of your core values this week.

## General Reflections:

One thing that struck me about this topic was: _____

_____

I'm still pondering *(and may seek more information on)*: _____

_____

As a result of this reflection, I plan to: _____

_____

_____

# Conversation 6

## Your Personal Mission

**Purpose:** A personal mission is a statement about your *why*. This is what drives you to get out of bed in the morning. It describes what you believe is most important in life, what you wish to focus on, and what you want to be known for. If you allow it to direct your thoughts and actions each day, it has the *potential* to direct your life and achieve the future you want.

I often tell my students to consider holding on to this paper. When one finds themself applying for a promotion or future job, having *(and referencing)* a personal mission can help them stand out from other candidates. Many graduate school applications request a personal philosophy and/or mission statement as well. This can be an excellent start.

## Four Steps to Your Personal Mission:

**1.** Think about your **Core Beliefs and Values.** Write down three or four key words or phrases under each of the following.

Core beliefs: What are some key things you believe?

Core values: What are some key things you value?

Overall, what really matters in life? What's most important?

**2. Hopes, Dreams, Desires, Goals:** Think about your hopes, dreams, desires, and goals. Write these based on current circumstances. Jot down two or three items under each category. These can be whatever comes into your mind. These are not commitments but *possibilities*.

Personal:

School/Career:

Community/World:

Family/Friends:

Spiritual:

**3. Leaving a Legacy:** These questions are to help focus your long-term thinking.

How would you like to be remembered? What one thing do you want people to say about you (now or after you're gone)? [Do not look back at your answer from Conversation 2 until you write your thoughts here. Then, look back and compare.]

What have you contributed to the world during your life so far? What do you dream of contributing in the future?

What steps can you begin to take to achieve your desired contributions, hopes, dreams, and goals?

**4. Drafting Personal Mission Statement:**

Review everything you've written so far. Circle or <u>underline</u> any words that stand out in your mind.

Using key words and ideas from above, write your mission. Don't worry about getting it perfect. Just get down the basics. Refine it later. It will evolve over time. You could begin with: *My mission in life is to...*

_____

_____

## You in Two Words:

You now have a draft mission. Try to quantify what it says in just two words. What are the two most important words that could define you?

1. _____ 2. _____

The signature line below is meaningful. It conveys the seriousness of missional living. Sign your name. Then live it.

Signed: _____ Date: _____

**Homework:** Do your friends, coworkers, and family members know these things about you? How might you begin to let others see and understand what is most important in your life? How might you share this newly written mission with others? Jot ideas down. Then do them.

## General Reflections:

One thing that struck me about this topic was: _____
_____

I'm still pondering *(and may seek more information on)*: _____
_____

As a result of this reflection, I plan to: _____
_____
_____

## Conversation 7

### Leveraging Gratitude

**Background:** The science of gratitude has expanded greatly in the past twenty years. Studies increasingly show that regularly practicing gratitude contributes to better relationships, decreased anxiety, and increased internal satisfaction. These bolster what Daniel Goleman labels emotional and social intelligence, key items for success in our careers and lives.

When we pause to focus on things we're grateful for, we shift our thinking from negative to positive. This can energize and reinvigorate us even on a bad day.

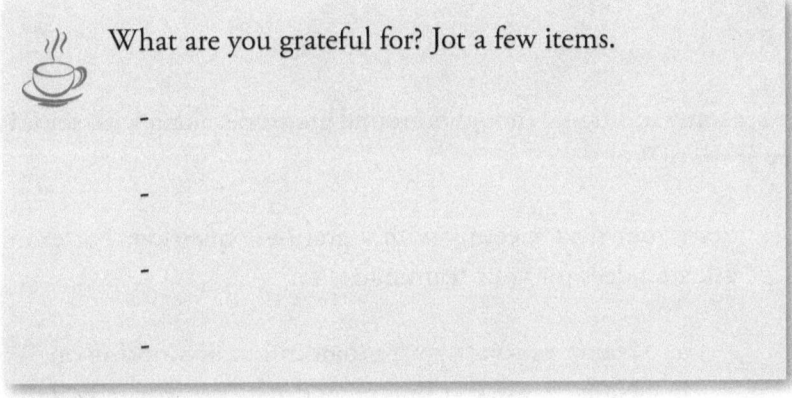

What are you grateful for? Jot a few items.

**The Challenge:** Could you increase your practice of gratitude? This may sound simple, but if you write down three things you are grateful for each day for twenty-one days, former Harvard researcher, Shawn Achor, says you will train your brain to look at the world differently. Once the habit is formed, you will start scanning the world for positives instead of threats. It's a game changer.

Researcher Robert Emmons, likewise, said that even though we do not have total control over our emotions, "being grateful is a choice that can sustain us through the ups and downs of our lives." When we become more grateful, we are more stress resistant and our self-worth increases.

This often shows outwardly. When that is noticed, it can result in career progression and success.

> Are you willing to take the 21-day gratitude test? (i.e., Will you write three things per day for which you're grateful?) ___Yes? ___ No? ___ Maybe
>
> How might increasing gratitude help your career? (Make a list of ideas here.)
>
> -
>
> -
>
> -

Here are some additional thoughts around gratitude, along with some ideas to try at the office:

1. Start your next meeting with a gratitude question. For example, ask attendees (or your teammates) to:

    a. Name a project you're thankful to be working on.
    b. Name a work colleague and tell how you're grateful for them.
    c. Describe a recent lesson you have learned, and how are you thankful for it.

2. In work situations, think about how you can be grateful for the person, not just their output.

3. Gratitude and appreciation go hand-in-hand. Review Dr. Gary Chapman's *5 Languages of Appreciation* (https://www.appreciationatwork.com/). Consider folks with whom you work, and how they prefer to receive gratitude. How might you show gratitude and appreciation for them this week?

**Homework:** Start and maintain a gratitude list. Keep it simple so it's not a chore. Carry it with you and refer to it weekly (at the very least). Try one of the three ideas above at your office.

**Additional Reading:** Dr. Gary Chapman's *5 Languages of Appreciation* (appreciationatwork.com)

## General Reflections:

One thing that struck me about this topic was: _____
_____

I'm still pondering *(and may seek more information on)*: _____
_____

As a result of this reflection, I plan to: _____
_____
_____

**Conversation 8**

## Building Curiosity

**Purpose:** Curiosity can help you make discoveries, identify paths when the way is unclear, and lead to learning. These are major predictors of success.

**The Discussion:** *What are you curious about?* Some folks will respond to this question with an immediate answer: "Everything!" Others may ask what you mean. Whether at one end of the spectrum or somewhere in the middle, how you respond to this question will help you consider how developing your curiosity can lead to long-term success.

In brief, curiosity is one of the most important traits and a high predictor for success identified by researchers at Korn Ferry, an international business consulting firm. In CEO Gary Burnison's Special Edition, *The Fall Whisper,* he says most people think of growth, strategy, and vision as key traits for leaders. But curiosity has recently become recognized as an absolutely critical piece.

Since the pandemic of 2020, Burnison says our world has experienced "nonstop ambiguity" which requires leaders to look at the world with an open mind. Whatever your organization (for profit, non-profit, education, government, etc.), today's rapid changes can only be met if we are aware of emerging trends and subsequently ready ourselves for action to meet the opportunities (or the risks) presented. We can meet this challenge by increasing our curiosity.

Here are three questions that can help increase curiosity:

1. What are you curious about right now?

   -

   -

   -

2. How might you increase your curiosity (in more areas of your work and life)?

   -

   -

   -

3. How might listening be a strategy for increasing your curiosity? (Think about that one for a few moments.)

   -

   -

To help with the questions above, think about context. Burnison says context is best friends with curiosity. By considering context, almost any event, trend, or observation can be handled or reframed to help visualize a path forward. By pairing curiosity with context and perspective, we can determine action. That is an invaluable skill.

**Summary:** In cultivating your curiosity, don't forget to expand your knowledge (and possible options) further by remembering to listen well. The saying that "experts don't listen because they already know the answer" rings true here. Imagine what might be missed if we are not open and curious to hear and learn about the other opportunities out there.

**Additional Reading:** Burnison, Gary (October 9, 2022). *The Fall Whisper.* Korn Ferry special edition publication.

## General Reflections:

One thing that struck me about this topic was: _____
_____

I'm still pondering *(and may seek more information on)*: _____
_____

As a result of this reflection, I plan to: _____
_____
_____

# Conversations for Deepening Connections

**Conversation 9**

## From Why? to What?

Let's just jump into this one. Think about the question below.

>  When bad news hits, can you change the question in your head from, "*Why* is this happening?" to "*What* can I learn?"
>
> Why might that be difficult? Jot down some ideas / thoughts.
>
> -
>
> -
>
> -

## My story:

"I am sorry Mr. Raison. You have cancer."

I heard nothing after that.

It was August 2014. I had gone in for a routine colonoscopy as screenings had become recommended for those aged fifty. But I knew how these things were supposed to go. If they find anything suspicious, the doctor says, "We found a small spot and have sent it out to the lab for a biopsy. We'll not even call unless there's a reason for a follow-up test."

Right? No doctor ever just walks in the room, sits down, looks you in the eye, and says, "You have cancer." That's not how it works. Or so I thought.

It's remarkable how many things can run through your mind in an instant. There is an explosion of thoughts—pictures of those you love, of your hopes and dreams, of questions like, "How long do I have?" After a few hours of settling down, one question emerges and lingers:

"*Why* is this happening to me?"

This is a legitimate question, and it is natural to ask it. It is also dangerous to remain in that space. Asking *why* does nothing helpful because *there is no answer*. Cancer happens.

And guess what? Job loss happens. As does stress. Emotional breakdown. Pain. Death. Or how about criticism? That can be extraordinarily painful. Write your own list. Better yet, don't. Instead, see if you can reframe the question and your thinking.

## The Switch:

When faced with a major life challenge or pain-point, here is one of the most powerful things a person can do:

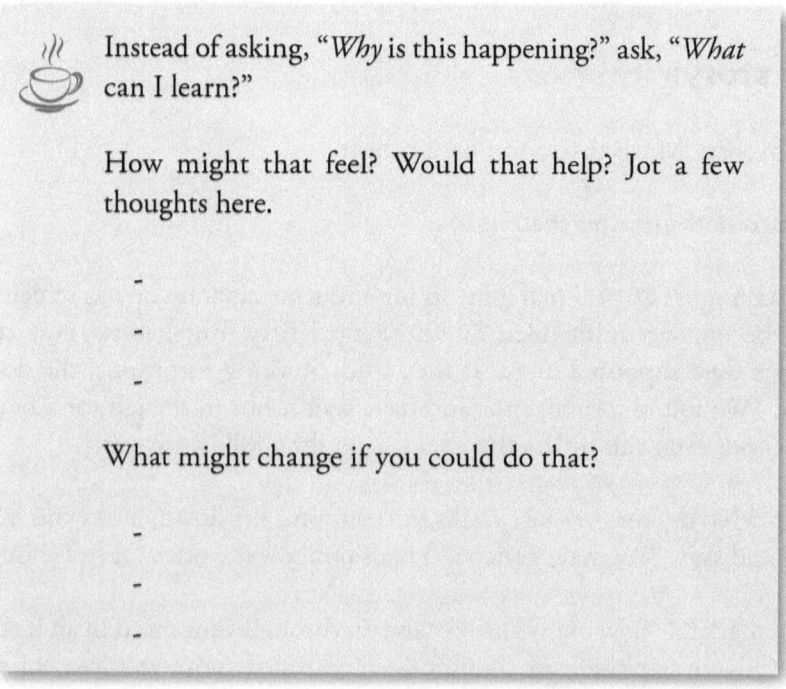

Instead of asking, "*Why* is this happening?" ask, "*What* can I learn?"

How might that feel? Would that help? Jot a few thoughts here.

- 
- 
- 

What might change if you could do that?

- 
- 
-

If you can shift your response from *why* to *what*, you can improve both your mental and physical health. They are intertwined.

**The Final Challenge:** The next time you experience a significant pain or stress point, and *after* you have changed the question from "*Why* is this happening?" to "*What* can I learn?" ask yourself this:

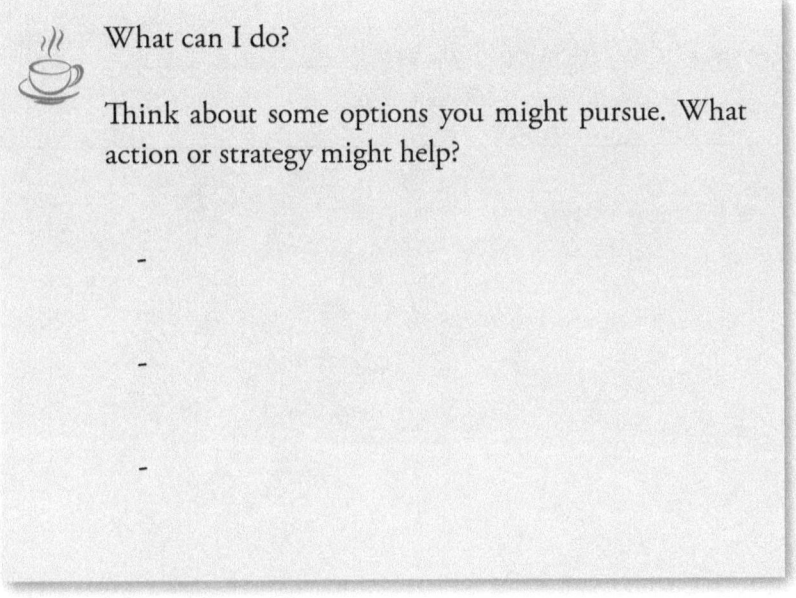

It's okay to take some time with this question. After my cancer diagnosis, I asked myself this question. That led to action (innovative surgery) that today, finds me still cancer-free after ten years. That gratitude is with me every single day.

**Homework:** The next time you encounter a trigger-event (at work, home, or play), *try to change the question in your head from Why to What.* Then consider sharing your burden, talking with friends, or making an appointment with a counselor. They can help. In my case, we took additional action to lower our mental stress by leaning into our family's faith tradition. Here, we found different, but significant comfort. Try moving from *why* to *what*. You'll be glad you did.

## General Reflections:

One thing that struck me about this topic was: _____
_____

I'm still pondering *(and may seek more information on)*: _____
_____

As a result of this reflection, I plan to: _____
_____
_____

**Conversation 10**

## Feeling Safe

**Background:** Do you feel safe right now in whatever living or work situation you find yourself? Think back to Maslow's hierarchy of needs. We need physiological foundations, then safety, love and belonging, esteem, and self-actualization. If most of our physiological needs are met, *safety* becomes the second-most foundational factor. Hence the question: *Do you feel safe?*

Please note: In this conversation, I am hoping to challenge you to think about how you can ground yourself in safety and comfort so that you can take a risk and grow personally or professionally. If you have any type of physical or mental situation that is unsafe right now, call someone immediately. Reach out for help. There are people who care about you. Do not hesitate here.

| Maslow's Hierarchy of Needs | |
|---|---|
| Self-actualization | Creativity, morality, problem solving, acceptance of facts, lack of prejudice |
| Self-esteem | Confidence, achievement, fulfillment |
| Love and belonging | Family, friendship, intimacy, connection |
| Safety and security | Physical (bodily) security, work, resources, morality, family, health |
| Physiological needs | Physical needs (air, water, food, sleep, reproduction, etc.) |

**Reflection:** Take just a moment to think about why you are talking with a mentor (or using this journal for self-growth). Then, ask yourself these questions.

Do you feel like you can be yourself in conversations with your mentor (or with a friend)?

Can you be yourself with yourself? Can you reflect on your own mistakes and imperfections?

Being honest, transparent, and authentic with ourselves and our mentors (or friends) goes a long way in building relationships. This helps us learn and grow.

**Homework:** This week, make a list of things that make you feel safe. Reflect on those items. Consider how that feeling of security can help you advance in your career (perhaps by giving yourself the courage to take a risk). As a challenge, consider how you might help a friend feel safe.

 Things that make me feel safe:

- 
- 
- 
- 
- 

Challenge: How can you help a friend who's struggling feel safe?

## General Reflections:

One thing that struck me about this topic was: _____
_____

I'm still pondering *(and may seek more information on)*: _____
_____

As a result of this reflection, I plan to: _____
_____
_____

**Conversation 11**

## What's Your Biggest Fear?
### *A Check-in for Mental Health*

**Purpose:** To help you reframe any issue and *see it from another perspective.* This is one of the most powerful things anyone can do. Changing our perspective can help us think through and positively respond to anxieties and stresses that we feel every day.

**Background:** For several years, I have done a classroom activity with my undergraduate students that begins by asking: "What's your biggest fear?" Each semester, I receive both funny and serious responses. Students write: "I'm afraid of spiders!" "Being eaten by a shark." "Vampires!" But many responses are deeper concerns: "Not doing well in my classes." "Never being enough." "Balancing my life." "Not living up to expectations." "Failure."

Give my question a try:

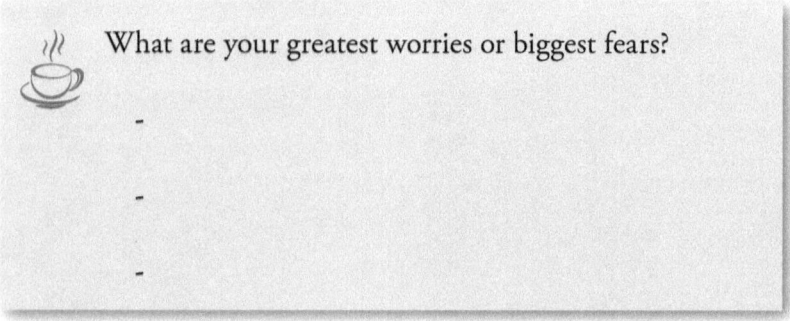

In class, I share their responses anonymously. When students see what their classmates wrote, there is a visceral response—a collective but quiet acknowledgement on each face in the room. You can see it. You can feel it. Then I ask a second question.

Please give this one a try:

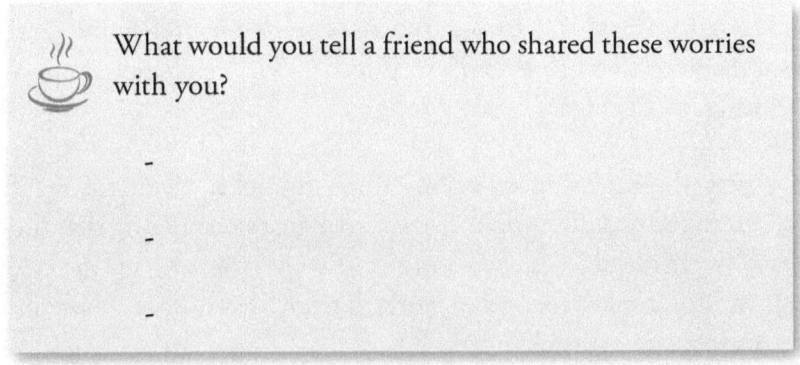

What would you tell a friend who shared these worries with you?

-

-

-

Each time I do this experiment, my students provide peer advice that is strengthening, encouraging, and hopeful. They recognize that sometimes, we need not give *any* advice, but simply sit and be with someone (or if physically distant, we let them know we are thinking of them and are available to listen at a moment's notice). My students have a remarkable ability to empathize and help each other. They have the answers! In shifting their perspective from *self* to *other*, it frees their mind to respond clearly with helpful suggestions.

But there's one more question, a reflective learning piece. This is the metacognition component. What do you think?

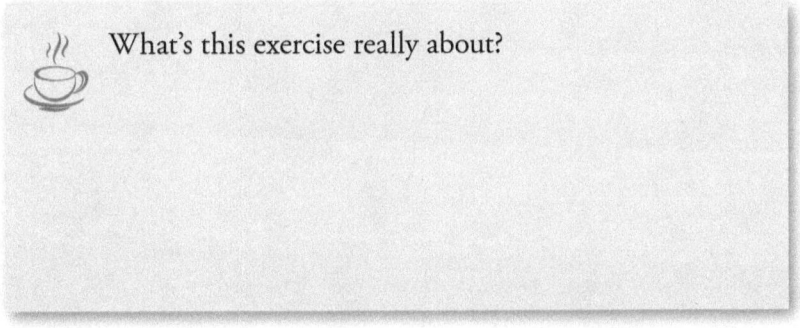

What's this exercise really about?

In class, my students immediately respond: "It showed us we're not alone." "We're not the only ones worried about stuff." "We can talk with friends and share our troubles." This solidifies the lesson in real time. This provides the perspective shift.

**The Challenge:** I always summarize the experiment. "Acknowledge our concerns and worries. They are legitimate. Find a licensed counselor or a friend to talk with when we need. But also, invest time reflecting on those beautiful things that bring comfort. Life is good. We are not alone. We'll get through all of this together."

Please give these closing questions some thought. They are my final questions to the class. The objective is to depart remembering that though we have worries and fears, we can find help by reflecting on the positive things in life. It takes focus and work. It's not always easy. But comfort, hope, and joy are game changers.

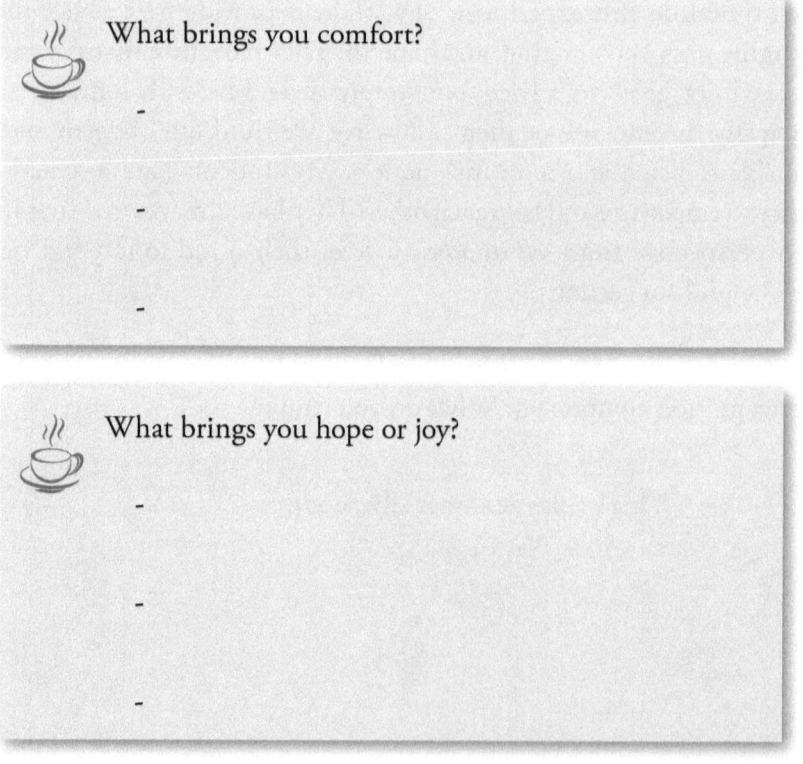

I hope you will give this experiment a try. It is a tremendously powerful reminder of how changing our perspective (from inward/self, to outward/other) can awaken insight and solutions.

## General Reflections:

One thing that struck me about this topic was: _____
_____

I'm still pondering *(and may seek more information on)*: _____
_____

As a result of this reflection, I plan to: _____
_____
_____

**Conversation 12**

## Bravery. Failure. Kindness.

**Purpose:** This conversation reminds us that bravery and failures occur every day, and that kindness is a mainstay which can be life changing for both the receiver and the giver.

**Background:** These three seemingly disparate concepts were beautifully woven together in a 2016 Huffington Post article in which author Meg Conley outlined the story of her concern with how to best help her children manage some of the struggles of youth. She came up with the idea of asking three questions:

- How can you be *brave* every day when facing an ever-changing world?
- How can you learn from *failure* and leverage that for later success?
- How can you be *kind*, even in the face of those who aren't so nice to you?

Notice anything? Yes. These questions are also germane to adults. But our responses and the subsequent implications may have greater stakes and significance.

I have done this exercise with my students. It resonates with them. Again, pausing to reflect is powerful. Here are the questions. Please take a few moments and jot down some of your thoughts.

| **3 Questions for Reflection** | |
|---|---|
| **Bravery:** | How were you brave today (or this week)? |
| **Failure:** | How did you fail today (or this week)? |
| **Kindness:** | How were you kind today (or this week)? |

**Question 1:** How were you brave today? Or how can one be brave every day when facing challenges of work, home, finances, and an ever-changing world? The key is to remember one thing: We are brave every day.

> *Bravery's Key Point:* We practice countless acts of bravery, but we do not hold them collective. If we can train our brains to recognize and remember small moments of bravery, we will have a tremendous tool (Archimedes' lever even) to deploy when something big happens and we need to be really brave.

**Question 2:** How did you fail today? Or, how one can learn from failure and leverage that for later success?

> *Failure's Key Point:* As adults, we know that life is filled with failures. Some are self-inflicted, others come from the outside. Small failures are data, but so are the big ones. If we remember this, we can turn failure into a

foundation, learning from and building on what did not work to subsequently find success.

**Question 3:** How were you kind today? Or, how can one be kind, even in the face of those who aren't so nice to you? This is a major challenge in life for many.

> *Kindness's Key Point:* Kindness is a mainstay. Acts of kindness bring joy to both the receiver and the giver. When we practice kindness, it can be life changing.

**Homework Challenge:** Try asking yourself these questions each day for one week. Write them on a scrap of paper and tape it on your bathroom mirror so you will see it each night. Then notice how you think about each. Pay attention to how your brain and body respond. How might you endeavor to bravely move forward to *what could be*? These questions can be powerful reminders of what matters and of the potential we all possess. And remember, you are brave in more ways than you know.

**Read more:** Conley, M. (2016). *Brave, Kind, Fail: We Ask Our Kids the Same 3 Questions Every Night.* Huffington Post Online 08/24/2016. Available at: https://www.huffpost.com/entry/we-ask-our-kids-the-same-3-questions-every-night_b_11665530

## General Reflections:

One thing that struck me about this topic was: _____
_____

I'm still pondering *(and may seek more information on)*: _____
_____

As a result of this reflection, I plan to: _____
_____
_____

**Conversation 13**

## Joy vs. Happiness: *Finding Fulfillment in Work and Life*

**Purpose:** To help you differentiate external, temporal happiness from internal, lasting joy. Could this help you survive *unhappy* moments in life (or undesirable job assignments at work)?

**The Discussion:** Dictionary.com suggests that being *happy* is "feeling or showing pleasure or contentment." When I hear that, I think of a moment or an event. But we have other words for deeper contentment. There, we think of words like fulfillment, satisfaction, and joy.

But have you ever found yourself saying, "I just want to be happy"? That's legit. It's real. And at times, it is tangible, particularly after a long week. It doesn't seem like too much of a request. But if happiness is focused on more external, materialistic pleasures, would it be better if we could shift our internal voice to say, "I just want to have joy"? Doing this moves us out of the temporal happiness into a long-term emotional well-being space.

Here are some questions to ponder:

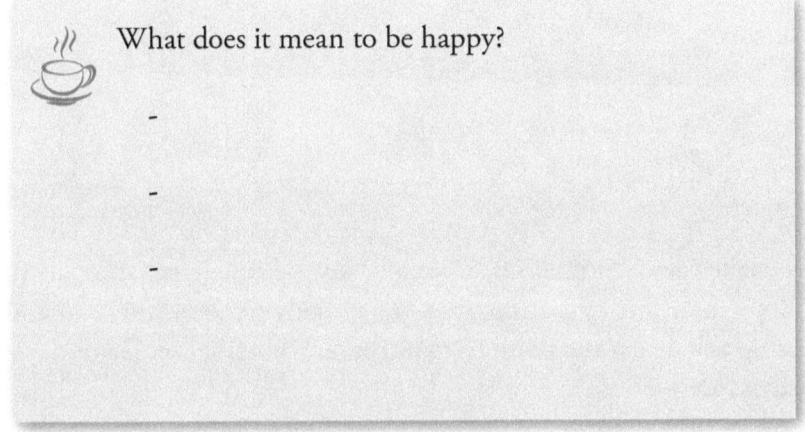

What does it mean to be happy?

-

-

-

*Conversations for Deepening Connections*

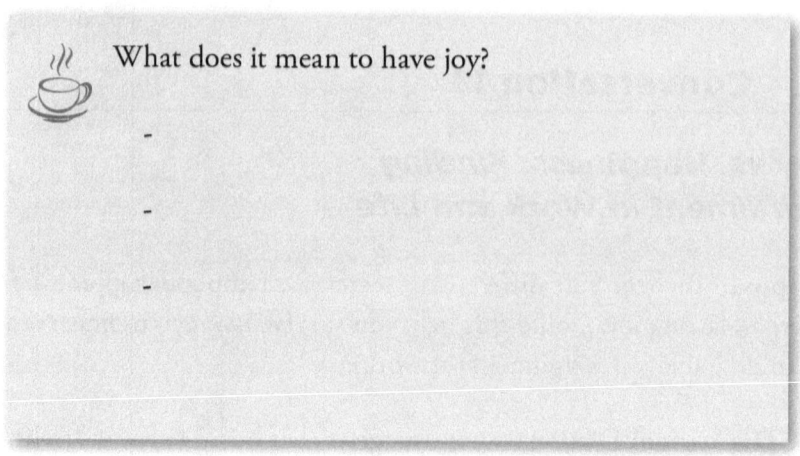

What does it mean to have joy?

-

-

-

Though nuanced, joy and happiness can be thought of very differently. Consider the differences you've outlined above, then respond to the question below:

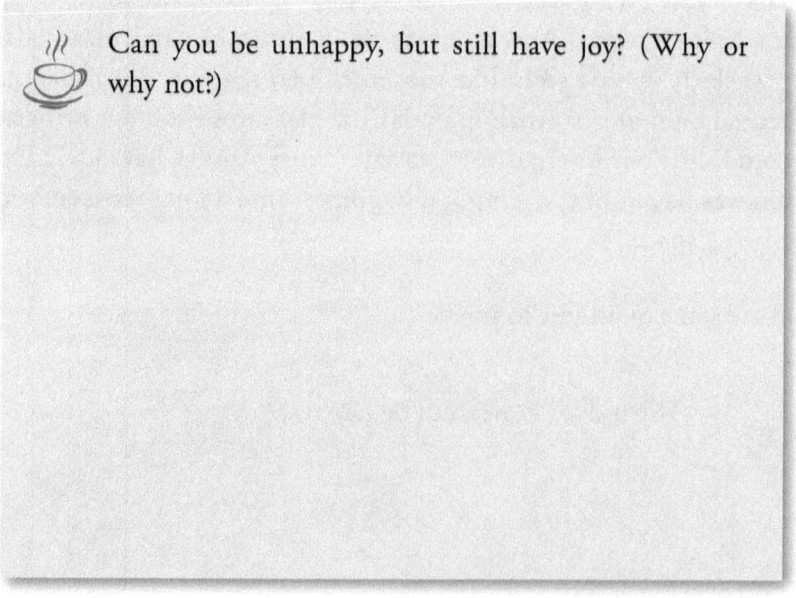

Can you be unhappy, but still have joy? (Why or why not?)

If we make these distinctions, we might just be able to get through those unhappy moments by leaning into our underlying joy which can endure hardship and trials, and point us to purpose. For a final application, please consider this:

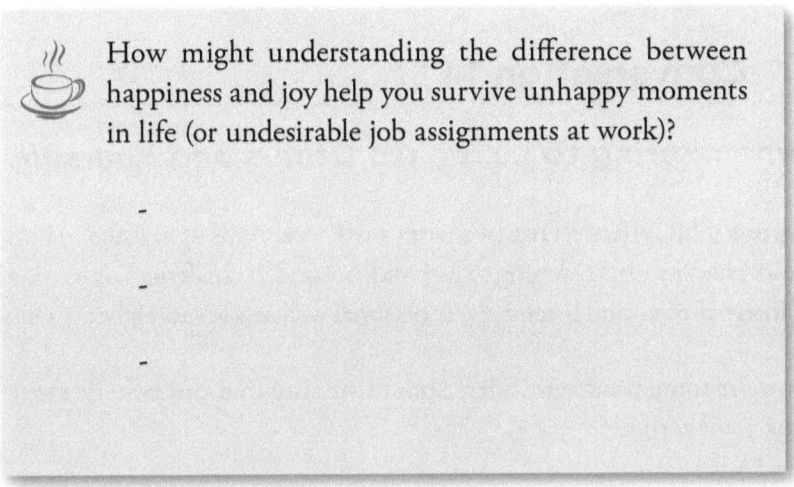

How might understanding the difference between happiness and joy help you survive unhappy moments in life (or undesirable job assignments at work)?

**For additional reading:** Dalai Lama XIV, Desmond Tutu, and Douglas Carlton Abrams. *The Book of Joy: Lasting Happiness in a Changing World.* New York: Avery, 2016.

## General Reflections:

One thing that struck me about this topic was: _____
_____

I'm still pondering *(and may seek more information on)*: _____
_____

As a result of this reflection, I plan to: _____
_____
_____

## Conversation 14

### Remembering to Listen *(to Others and Yourself)*

**Purpose:** This reflection has two parts. First, it reminds us to listen to hear and to understand versus listening to respond. Second, it challenges us to tune into our internal voice and listen for our personal wellness across eight dimensions.

Below are some basic reminders about listening that can benefit everyone. Please review these.

**Listening to Others:** Reminders on How to Listen for Understanding

>**Attitude:** Check your stress levels. Smile. A deliberate attitude check can change any conversation. Focus on the person before you.

>**Attend:** *Verbal attending* is when you practice intently listening without interruption, questions, or introducing new topics.

>**Close reflection:** When you restate key ideas using the same words as much as possible, you show that you are closely listening to their description of an event or concern. It can also show that you are honoring their history, background, or culture, further building connection and trust.

>**Insightful reflection:** Look for ways to express the essential feelings that are said or hinted at. But do not assume too much. Use questions in your reflecting response to clarify or to go deeper.

>**Paraphrase:** Summarizing can help you see if you really understand before continuing.

**Focus:** Pick out a key idea and ask for clarification. "You have been talking about several concerns. Which is most important to you?"

**Summary:** While we tend to know most of these things, we often forget or even fail to bring them to our conscious mind when we are supposedly listening. Being mindful is critical.

**Listening to Yourself:** 8 Dimensions of Wellness

**Background:** As we work to improve how we listen to others, we also need to consider how we listen to ourselves, particularly in the area of wellness. Please consider each dimension and its definition below. Then, jot a few ideas in the boxes to the right answering the prompt question.

| Listening to Yourself: *8 Dimensions of Wellness* | |
|---|---|
| **Dimension Category:** | How are you doing in this dimension right now? (Listen to your internal voice. What is it saying to you?) |
| **Career** – You gain personal satisfaction in your work consistent with your values, goals, and lifestyle. | |
| **Digital** – You consider the impact of your virtual presence and use of technology on your overall well-being. | |

| | |
|---|---|
| **Emotional** – You can identify, express, and manage the entire range of feelings (e.g., coping with stress). | |
| **Financial** – You know your financial state. You budget, save, and manage finances to achieve realistic goals. | |
| **Intellectual** – You value lifelong learning and seek to foster critical thinking. | |
| **Physical** – The physically well person gets adequate sleep, eats a nutritious diet, engages in exercise. | |
| **Social** – You have a network of support based on interdependence, mutual trust, respect. | |
| **Spiritual** – You seek harmony and balance by openly exploring the depth of human purpose. | |

**Internal Listening Challenge:** Look at your responses above. Consider how you are doing in each dimension. Now jot down some ideas on the question below.

| What advice would you give a friend who had questions or was struggling in some of the above *8 Dimensions*? What could you tell them to help? ||
|---|---|
| **Dimension:** | **Advice:** |
|  |  |
|  |  |
|  |  |
|  |  |

**Summary:** You may, of course, realize that the advice you offer a friend in the box above is likely applicable in your own life. That's the beauty of reflection. Now, look back at your initial responses to the eight dimensions. Which ones might be a struggle for you? What advice would a friend offer you? Changing our perspective allows us to help ourselves.

## General Reflections:

One thing that struck me about this topic was: _____

I'm still pondering *(and may seek more information on)*: _____

As a result of this reflection, I plan to: _____

# Conversations for Career Advancement

## Conversation 15

### Who You Are *vs.* What You Do

**Purpose:** To help you think about who you are or who you want to become instead of the classic question which asks what you want *to do*.

**Background:** What is the one thing people almost always asked you when you were young? For many, we heard the repeated question, "What do you want to be when you grow up?" Some of us imagined firefighting, others considered becoming a nurse, farmer, or teacher.

Asking "Who do you want to become?" is qualitatively different from the normal inquiries we get as children about what we want to be. Many of us were never encouraged to really think through what we enjoy doing, what we are good at (natural gifts), and where we want to learn more. When coupled with what is needed (in business, society, the home, etc.), this is a trifecta that can point to future career satisfaction.

The question below is one many people have never been asked. It is the opposite of what we've been trained to expect. (i.e., What is your next career move? What position are you hoping to attain?) The question may take a moment to sink in. Give yourself time in responding. (Please jot some ideas below before looking back at Conversation 3 which asks a variation of this same question. Again, this is purposeful in helping you create the future you want.)

 Who do you want to become?

**Summary:** You do not need to fully answer this question right now, on the spot. Jot some ideas down. Then ponder it over the coming days and weeks. Then expand your writing. Also, look back and reflect on the *Personal Mission* and *Five Things* exercises.

**Challenge question:** This is a way to think about how to achieve the *who* you want to become.

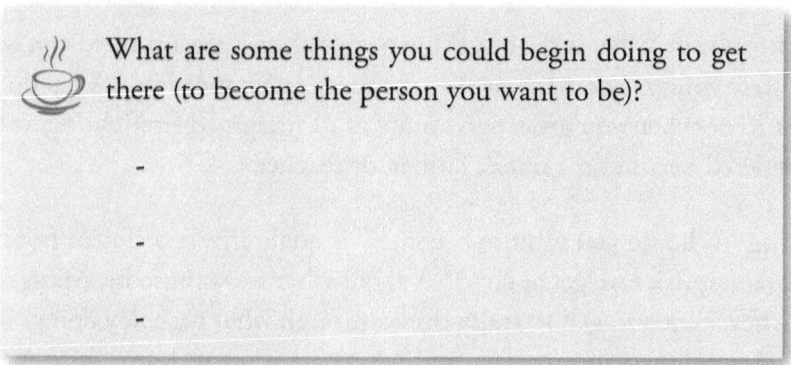

What are some things you could begin doing to get there (to become the person you want to be)?

-
-
-

**Note:** This is a question that you may wish to return to over the course of completing this journal. Feel free to do that with any of the questions. Your answers will change, and that's normal. This is a journey. This is the journey of your life.

## General Reflections:

One thing that struck me about this topic was: _____
_____

I'm still pondering *(and may seek more information on)*: _____
_____

As a result of this reflection, I plan to: _____
_____
_____

**Conversation 16**

## What Motivates You?

**Purpose:** This reflection is designed to help you understand the basic premise of motivation. It begins by asking a simple question:

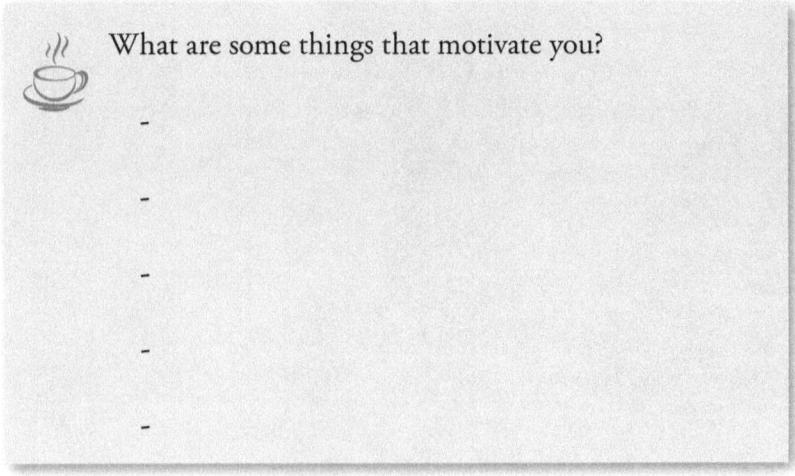

At the most basic level, humans are driven by two forms of motivation: *intrinsic* and *extrinsic*. Extrinsic motivators come from the outside and include things like money, power and prestige, and where you work. Here, people pursue the goal simply because of the visible, external reward or punishment. Intrinsic motivators (such as gaining knowledge, mastery, curiosity, autonomy, or fulfillment) come from within. People pursue these because they enjoy the work and find some kind of inherent satisfaction that feeds their life purpose or mission.

Author Susan Fowler outlines four components that *intrinsic* motivation has in the workplace:

- **Competence:** you have the necessary skills to perform work / activities

- **Meaning:** your work goal or purpose aligns with your personal ideals or standards
- **Autonomy:** you have some level of control over your choices or behaviors
- **Impact:** you can influence the strategy, administration, or outcomes

Question for reflection:

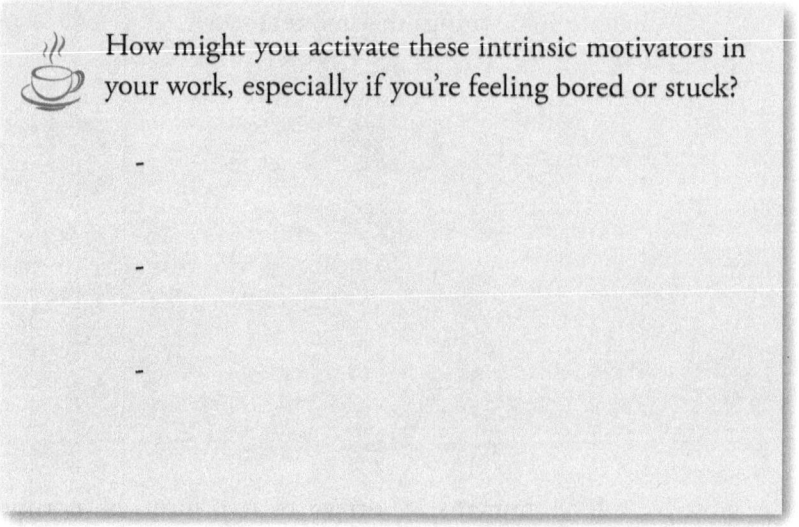

How might you activate these intrinsic motivators in your work, especially if you're feeling bored or stuck?

-

-

-

Here are two strategies that might help.

1. Find ways to make tasks more interesting. Ask your supervisor if you could try different projects to add variety to your work.

2. Think about how your work has meaning. Ask yourself how it can have a substantial impact on the lives and work of other people. Make a mental link between your specific job tasks and your organization's mission. This is powerful.

**Challenge:** Jot down a few items over the next week or so that come to mind about your motivations. Separate them by category. Which ones feel stronger? Which ones resonate with your soul?

| My Meaningful Motivation List: |
|---|
| Intrinsic:<br><br>- <br>- <br>- <br>- <br>- <br><br><br>Extrinsic:<br><br>- <br>- <br>- <br>- <br>- |

**Homework:** Return to this list on occasion. Pick out one or two motivators. Then set a goal to try and increase your focus on those meaningful items.

## General Reflections:

One thing that struck me about this topic was: _____
_____

I'm still pondering *(and may seek more information on)*: _____
_____

As a result of this reflection, I plan to: _____
_____
_____

# Conversation 17

## Change. Growth Mindset. Ambiguity. Three Skills for Career Advancement

**Purpose:** To help you consider three critical skills that, if communicated and demonstrated, will help you capture the attention of your supervisor (or a hiring manager) and help propel your career advancement.

Before jumping in though, let's set a foundation. Please reflect on this simple, but deep question:

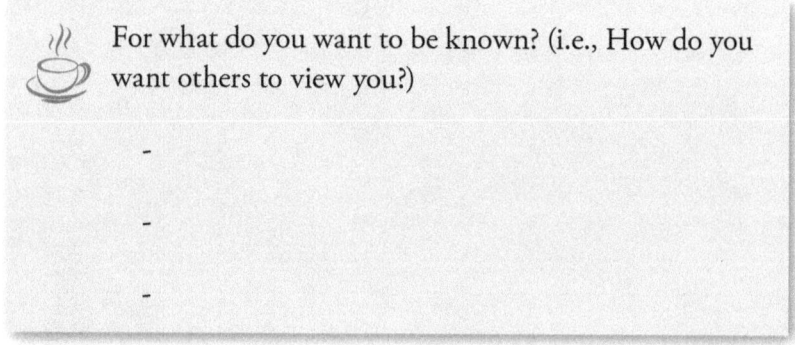

For what do you want to be known? (i.e., How do you want others to view you?)

-

-

-

Now, as you consider how you want others to view you, think about how that might match up with an idea from Gary Burnison, Korn Ferry CEO, who outlines three critical professional skills that can help people advance in their career. These will help anyone stand out in an organization. Think about these three areas below. How are you at:

1. **Handling Change:** When change hits our workplaces (or lives), is our attitude one of immediate resistance? Or do we engage our curiosity and wonder? e.g., "Could this result in something good?"

2. **Growth Mindset:** Carol Dweck's research suggests people with a growth mindset believe that, even if they struggle with certain skills, their abilities are not set in stone. They understand that with work, their skill sets can grow and improve over time.

3. **Ambiguity:** Burnison defines dealing with ambiguity as knowing how to "make good decisions based on limited knowledge, or the information you have at the time." This takes some guts. Deciding and acting without knowing the whole picture can be frightening. But one can learn to gather information from diverse sources, weigh data, and mitigate risk and uncertainty.

Jot down some ideas around your skill or approach (or need for help) on these three topics:

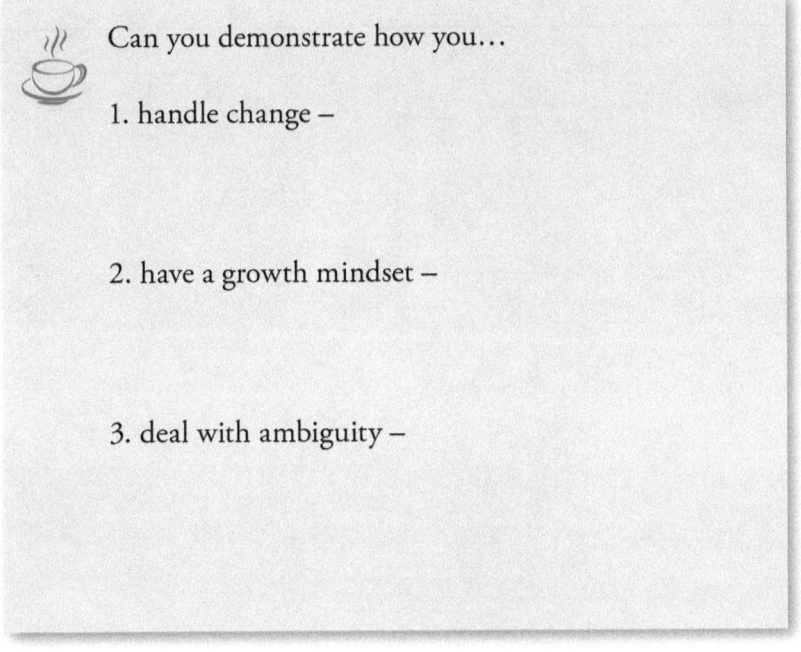

Can you demonstrate how you...

1. handle change –

2. have a growth mindset –

3. deal with ambiguity –

**Homework:** Seek training or conversation on any topic above where you need help. Look for places to lean in and use skills that you have in other areas. Demonstrating these will open opportunities.

**Sources:** Burnison, Gary (October 16, 2022). Special Edition. *Our Time to Take Control.*

Dweck, C. S. (2006). Mindset: The new psychology of success. Random House.

## General Reflections:

One thing that struck me about this topic was: _____
_____

I'm still pondering *(and may seek more information on)*: _____
_____

As a result of this reflection, I plan to: _____
_____
_____

## Conversation 18

### Reframing Six Stages of a Career
### *(from Ladder to Scaffold)*

**Purpose:** To help you gain an understanding of six elements that can direct a self-fulfilling career path. It's much more than climbing the proverbial corporate ladder.

**Background & Discussion:** You can easily find quotes from successful people including athletes, actors, and corporate giants who have said something like this: "I spent all this time climbing to the top; but when I got there, it felt meaningless, and I discovered I was all alone." So what might be an alternate ending? Is there a different and better path?

Here is a reframing question to consider:

 Instead of climbing the corporate (or non-profit, education, government, etc.) ladder alone, what if you invest in career growth while also encouraging and helping others along the way? What might that look like?

-

-

-

Korn Ferry CEO Gary Burnison outlines six phases of a career that offer growth and opportunity at each level. Imagine yourself moving through these. What does that look like?

1. **Follower:** These are usually the early years, a first, second, or third job, often just out of college. Burnison notes, "You will never lead if you don't know how to follow someone!"

2. **Collaborator:** You establish and demonstrate your strengths (check out Gallup's "Strength Finder"). You are still "operating from your technical skill set," but this will allow you to develop critical skills with people and teams.

3. **Instructor:** Still early in your career, you will find opportunities to lead and offer instructions to others (individually or on a team). Here, try to operate from both your technical and people skill sets. Use outside collaborators so you can learn too. The earnest teacher learns more than the student.

4. **Manager:** Officially managing people includes adding skills on motivation and mission. You may be setting goals and objectives or providing strategy. Review Simon Sinek's Start with Why. Encourage folks to think about mission every day.

5. **Influencer:** This is not social media, but a legitimate platform to begin leveraging your technical and people skills for positive impact.

6. **Leader:** This level may arise sooner than you expect. And not everyone is ready for it. Here, your time is invested in empowering and inspiring others. Burnison posits the idea that the leader is *no longer telling people* what to do, but is *providing guidance* on what to think about, and motivating them to reach their potential. (Please read that last sentence twice.)

Here are some questions to prompt your thinking and reflection:

1. What phase (1-6 above) might you be on right now?

2. Do you wish to advance? What might you do to position yourself?

3. How might having a plan or vision of your future help you create a positive and contributory career path?

**Summary:** Studies have shown that compensation and work-life balance are highly desired by today's workers. Opportunities for career growth and influence often rank as high, particularly with today's emerging workforce. What matters most in your vision of an intrinsically satisfying career?

Here is a second reframing question to consider. Considerations such as this can help you become a stronger leader.

Imagine your career as a scaffold that provides strong support and, unlike a ladder, allows more than one person on the platform at a time. How might that accelerate your personal or professional advancement?

-

-

-

**See also:** Burnison, G. (no date). 6 Stages of Career Growth: Where are you? Korn Ferry. https://www.kornferry.com/insights/this-week-in-leadership/six-stages-of-career-growth

## General Reflections:

One thing that struck me about this topic was: _____
_____

I'm still pondering *(and may seek more information on)*: _____
_____

As a result of this reflection, I plan to: _____
_____
_____

**Conversation 19**

## Handling Critics and Criticism:
*A Growth Mindset Approach*

**Purpose:** To help you build resilience and leverage critiques and criticism for good.

**Background:** Have you ever felt the gut-punch of a poor annual evaluation? Or have you had so much red ink on a paper it was hard to see what you originally wrote? How might you reframe this kind of feedback from critiques and critics without giving up or feeling beaten up? Could you leverage the input to help you grow? Here's a question to consider:

 How do you currently handle input (feedback, criticism, red ink) from critiques and critics? What is your initial reaction?

-

-

-

Many people hear feedback as outright criticism that is pointing directly at them as a person. While some critics are throwing darts you, *meaningful* evaluation or feedback is aimed at the work, not the person. Here are two-steps outlining how to receive a critique:

1. Remove yourself from the equation. Even if the criticism appears (or is) aimed directly at you. Change the words in your head from, "I'm no good at this," to, "This is something I still need to learn," or, "This is a critique aimed at helping improve this work."

2. Dispassionately use the input to find areas for improvement. Look at each suggestion (critique), evaluate how it might help, and then begin making changes for improvement.

**Adopt a Growth Mindset:** Carol Dweck (2008) identified a *fixed mindset* as only focusing on the outcome, and telling yourself you cannot change anything. Conversely, with a *growth mindset*, you realize the *critiques or criticisms are data that can help you* tackle problems, chart a new or redirected course, and continue working for success.

## 4 keys to Growth Mindset:

1. Believe that your *effort* leads to achievements. It's not just inherent talent.
2. Be willing to learn from mistakes. Leverage criticism as input to improve.
3. Know that intelligence and ability can be developed (again, through effort, grit, determination).
4. Embrace asking questions. Ask for help when needed. And admit when you don't know something.

Look at the 4 Keys above. Then consider this:

Which *key* above resonates with you? (It might resonate by making you feel positive, or one of them might make you feel angry.)

What might you do to improve in this area? Key #: _____

Action:

**Summary:** We *will* on occasion receive input, feedback, evaluation, and criticism that feels like a gut-punch. Everyone does. But changing the *aim* of the critique (from *me* to *my work*) and adopting a growth mindset can powerfully redirect the situation (and our emotions), leading to improved output.

**Important Postscript:** There are critics who may attack *you* personally. Those people are not interested in helping. You do not owe them your attention. Every single person has value and worth, regardless of skills (or ability to do some specific task). So if someone belittles you, take leave. Find an encourager who can help you get back on track and make the improvements you want to make. Then, pass it along and encourage someone else.

**Additional Reading:** Dweck, C. S. (2008). Mindset: The New Psychology of Success. New York: Ballantine Books.

## General Reflections:

One thing that struck me about this topic was: _____
_____

I'm still pondering *(and may seek more information on)*: _____
_____

As a result of this reflection, I plan to: _____
_____
_____

**Conversation 20**

## Providing Clarity

**Purpose:** To help you understand how providing clarity to work situations can make you indispensable.

**Background:** Researchers Jim Kouzes and Barry Posner outlined *5 Practices of Exemplary Leadership* based on years of research with thousands of organizations. Those practices are:

1. Model the Way
2. Inspire a Shared Vision
3. Challenge the Process
4. Enable Others to Act
5. Encourage the Heart

They have also asked people around the globe what they want in a leader. Overwhelmingly, the responses are *honesty, forward-looking, inspiring, and competent*. Three of these are rooted in the construct of *credibility*. Kouzes and Posner say *personal credibility* is the foundation of leadership.

 How would you define credibility in your own words?

Leadership guru Andy Stanley cites integrity as a number one leadership characteristic people want. Though nuanced, *credibility* and *integrity* are quite similar to the point that they could be labeled synonyms. Consider this:

How would you define integrity in your own words?

**The Discussion:** Stanley says people don't actually follow people because of their integrity. We do indeed *value* integrity and credibility, *but we follow clarity*. We follow the person who can outline a simple, clear path forward. He notes, "Clarity results in influence which is the essence of leadership." He contends clarity is magnetic. Clarity is about the future.

**Key point:** If someone can provide clarity, especially in problem identification, planning, or vision casting, they will be followed.

 What opportunities to provide clarity might you identify? Hint: Think about summarizing a conversation or a meeting (e.g., with a short bullet point memo). What else?

 How might your supervisor or team members view this kind of clarifying input?

Finally, consider this last challenge question.

 How could honing your ability to provide clarity propel your career advancement?

 Where might you apply this idea? i.e., Is there a team or project where you could offer clarity to assist in attaining the objective(s)?

**Sources:** Kouzes, J.M. & Posner, B.Z. (2012). The Leadership Challenge (5th ed.). John Wiley & Sons.

Stanley, Andy (2016). *Making Vision Stick*. Leadercast 2016: Architects of Tomorrow. Available at: https://youtu.be/zAOg_rGVlr4

## General Reflections:

One thing that struck me about this topic was: _____
_____

I'm still pondering *(and may seek more information on)*: _____
_____

As a result of this reflection, I plan to: _____
_____
_____

**Conversation 21**

## Triangulating Your Skills, Abilities, and Interests to Find Your Future

**Purpose:** To help you think through three items: 1.) what you enjoy doing, 2.) what you are good at (i.e., natural gifts), and 3.) where you want to learn more. Bringing these three together can powerfully steer you toward your desired future.

**The Discussion:** Most people have multiple gifts. Many people have the ability to do a variety of jobs, and career paths are frequently not linear. Anecdotally, my friends and former students share that their journeys have been directed more by chance than any kind of plan. That's okay if you are lucky. But many folks find themselves in ho-hum jobs they could take or leave.

So how can you change this approach?

I mentioned in Conversation 3 that we often prompt children to think about their future and possible professions by asking that age-old question: "What do you want to do when you grow up?" But even if they have taken some high school career assessments, the Myers-Briggs, or other employment interest instrument, many younger people have never thought through what they enjoy doing, what they are good at (natural gifts), and where they want to learn more. As I noted before, when coupled with what is needed (in business, society, the home, etc.), this is the trifecta that can point to future career satisfaction.

**The Process:** Consider these questions. Jot down a few ideas under each. Then review this list and consider it over the next few weeks. When answering these questions, do so in the context of considering your future career or *potential* employment:

☕ Skills, abilities, interests:

1. What do you enjoy doing?
   -

   -

   -

2. What are you good at (natural gifts)?
   -

   -

   -

3. What do you want to learn more about?
   -

   -

   -

**Summary:** This simple exercise can help you begin directing your career path while simultaneously aligning it with personal interests and life goals.

Challenge question:

> Imagine bringing those three things together. What field or job might you aim for in the future?
>
> -
>
> -
>
> -

## General Reflections:

One thing that struck me about this topic was: _____
_____

I'm still pondering *(and may seek more information on):* _____
_____

As a result of this reflection, I plan to: _____
_____
_____

## Conversation 22

### The Resume & Cover Letter: *Always be Prepared*

**Purpose:** To encourage you to be ready for job opportunities by keeping an updated resume, and to help you understand how recruiters and employers use AI to sort job applications.

**Background:** There is a lot of advice out there on designing resumes and cover letters. The key is to be clear. Be succinct. The main thing today's applicants need to understand is that they must get past the AI (artificial intelligence) that is doing the initial (and sometimes secondary) screening for almost every job. Applicant tracking systems (ATS) have been in wide use for quite a while and are becoming more sophisticated. Your objective is to have the right mix of keywords without going overboard so a real person will give your resume a look.

Whether you're seeking a job right now or not, it's good to have your resume ready. Here are two starting questions.

 What could help your resume get past first and second rounds of AI screening? (Think about highlights, clarity, cogent work descriptions.)

-
-
-

What keywords / highlights from your experience might you include?

-
-
-

Here are some additional tips that might help.

1. **Do not use columns** in your resume. It may or may not confuse AI or screen readers.

2. **Capture attention.** Write yourself a tag line. Include pertinent details. Capture the eight seconds of attention you're afforded when a human eye actually reviews your document. Pull them in.

 What's your tag line? (Hint: Look back at your *Five Things* and the *Personal Mission* reflections. These will contain your key words to deploy here.)

3. **Be judicious** in your attempt to game the system. Yes, match keywords in the position description with keywords in your resume. But don't go overboard. Advancements in AI can recognize gaming.

4. **Return to the fundamentals.** By this, I mean write your resume to tell your story. After you get past the AI, a real person will recognize a person who has real-life experience, AND who has reflected on it to understand what they have learned and how they can apply that in their next position.

   Here's an example I've seen from numerous students when I'm reviewing their documents:

   They list: "Server at X restaurant."

   They should rephrase: "Used my creative thinking and problem identification skills to recognize customer needs and respond to create a positive experience." (This rephrase tells the reader that you actually thought about what you were doing, and how it could make a positive difference for the restaurant. This is extraordinarily better than simply listing the task you performed. This shows metacognition. This will bolster any resume entry.)

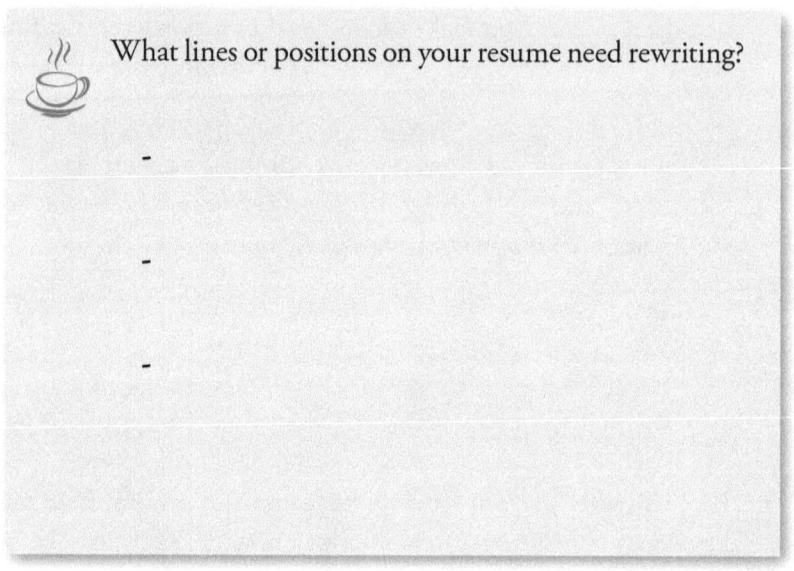

What lines or positions on your resume need rewriting?

-

-

-

**Summary:** Know that AI will be screening your resume. Create one that will advance you to the next step so your real self and ability can shine.

## General Reflections:

One thing that struck me about this topic was: _____
_____

I'm still pondering *(and may seek more information on)*: _____
_____

As a result of this reflection, I plan to: _____
_____
_____

**Conversation 23**

### Real Interview Tips that Work

**Purpose:** This conversation will help you think about key points in preparing for a potential career-changing interview.

**Background:** Throughout my career, I have interviewed hundreds of people for positions ranging from entry-level laborers to executives (including corporate, non-profit, and higher education leaders with earned doctorates). For over thirty-five years in my various jobs, I've observed several key points worth sharing.

I strongly encourage folks to read through tips on LinkedIn, Handshake, and other job boards. But then, I challenge them to consider where they are now, and whether they're ready for an interview.

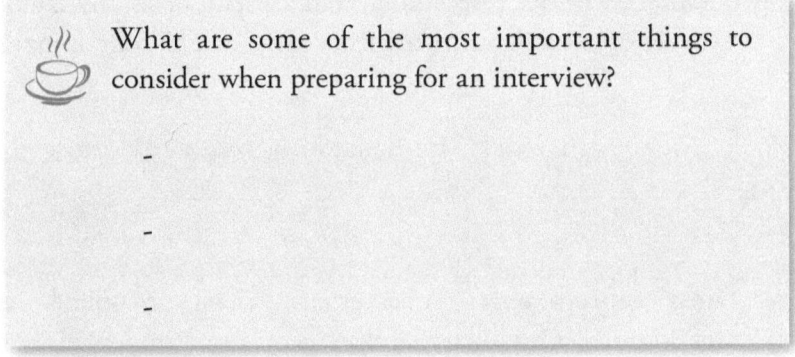

What are some of the most important things to consider when preparing for an interview?

-

-

-

This is a tricky question because, arguably, there is no correct answer. Please read on. I outline some basics below.

**Preparation to Ensure Success:** The purpose of an interview is to showcase your skills, experience, and personality to a hiring manager or team in a short amount of time. That window may be in person, or online. This can be stressful but managed with some simple preparation. Here are the basics:

1. **Research the company:** Learn all about the job and the company. Know their mission, history, products, and services. The best candidates I have ever interviewed were those who related their *personal mission* to our *corporate mission*.

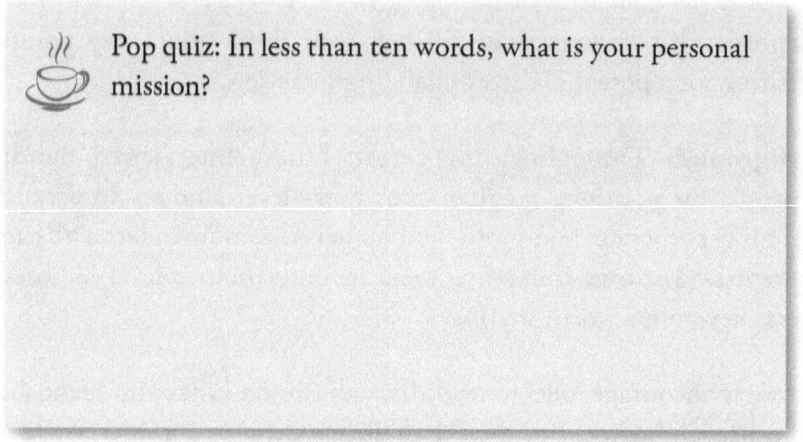

Pop quiz: In less than ten words, what is your personal mission?

2. **Practice your responses:** Be familiar with common interview questions. Practice responding with a friend or family member. Articulate your skills and experience in a clear and concise manner.

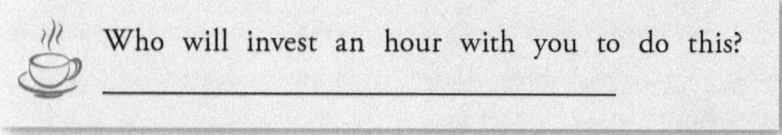

Who will invest an hour with you to do this?

3. **Dress appropriately:** Whether in person or online, dress professionally. Our society judges people on *first impressions*. If online, position your camera to frame a positive background or scene.

4. **Be on time:** Arrive on time or log in early. This punctuality shows your respect for the interviewer's time.

5. **Listen:** Instead of formulating responses in your mind, listen carefully to the interviewer's questions. Feel free to pause, reflect, and then provide examples of your experience.

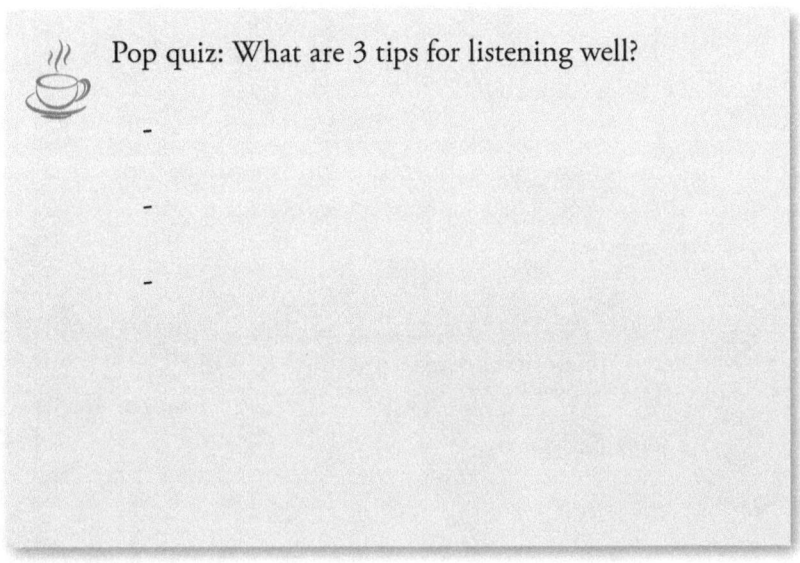

Pop quiz: What are 3 tips for listening well?

-

-

-

6. **Follow up:** After the interview, send a thank you email or note to the interviewer.

These six tips are rather generic, but there is the one key that is sometimes missed:

> During the interview, you must convey how your education, experience, and personal mission align with their corporate mission. Say aloud: "I want my work to help move (the organization) toward your mission of x, y, z." (Fill in with their mission brief.)

Connecting your personal mission to their corporate mission will greatly enhance your potential of landing the job. You are demonstrating your understanding of the proverbial big picture, not just a task that you know how to do or a discipline in which you have a degree.

> A lot of interviews will open with this: "Tell us a little bit about yourself."
>
> **Challenge:** How will you begin your response? (This is key. You need to have a clear, strong opener.) For example:
>
> I want to help _____ (organization) accomplish its bottom-line mission of _____ _____ (2 or 3 words from their mission) by…
>
> - 
>
> - 
>
> - 

**Summary:** Even if you are not actively looking for a new job, if you consciously work to demonstrate how your professional mission supports your organization's mission, you may receive offers or promotions that you had not even thought about.

## General Reflections:

One thing that struck me about this topic was: _____
_____

I'm still pondering *(and may seek more information on)*: _____
_____

As a result of this reflection, I plan to: _____
_____
_____

**Conversation 24**

### The Stay Interview: *Is Staying an Opportunity?*

**Purpose:** To help you gain a larger vision of why and how staying can be a positive contribution to your employer and can help advance your career. These questions can also be considered to determine if changing jobs might be beneficial.

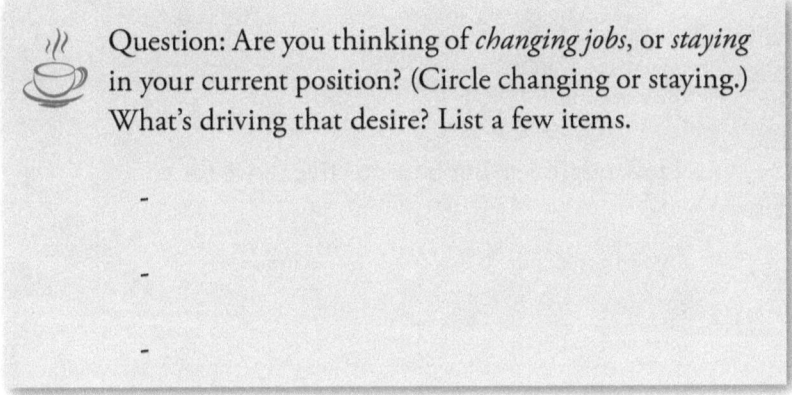

Question: Are you thinking of *changing jobs*, or *staying* in your current position? (Circle changing or staying.) What's driving that desire? List a few items.

-

-

-

**Background:** Employee turnover rates have increased dramatically in recent years. Blame it on COVID, the gig economy, pay/benefit differentials, metal health stressors, generational change, or life balance, but turnover is real. For companies, turnover has direct costs in time (hiring process, onboarding, new people becoming effective) and dollars (customer/order loss, unemployment costs, etc.). Retaining good employees also contributes to institutional knowledge that can benefit an organization.

Employees sometimes look to change jobs to get ahead. But could staying be a career advancement strategy?

These questions are based on Richard Finnegan's seminal idea of the *stay interview* that seeks to learn what actions can improve employee engagement and retention. But the questions below can help you gain insight around your current position and help you consider opportunities that might avail themselves by staying in your current job. They might also help you make a decision for leaving it. Investing time in thinking this through is key.

**The Questions:** Jot down a few ideas around each of these.

 How might staying in your current role open opportunities for advancement?

How might leaving be a positive move for you?

 Organizations are seeing increased turnover. What opportunities may exist if you stay?

-

-

-

Consider these questions *regardless of your interest in staying or changing jobs*. These will help you think about potential career advancement either way.

| | The Self-Interview: |
|---|---|
| 1. | What do you look forward to when you come to work each day? |
| 2. | What do you like least about your work? |
| 3. | What might tempt you to leave? |
| 4. | If you could change something about your job, what would that be? |
| 5. | What talents are not being used in your current role? |
| 6. | Are there other positions at your current organization that you could aim for advancement? |

In total, these questions are keys that can help you understand where you currently see yourself in an organization, and then evaluate whether leaving or staying might be strategic in advancing your career. Consider them carefully. Revisit these in a week or two. Then, ask yourself what's changed or what has become solidified in your mind.

## General Reflections:

One thing that struck me about this topic was: _____
_____

I'm still pondering *(and may seek more information on)*: _____
_____

As a result of this reflection, I plan to: _____
_____
_____

**Conversation 25a - *Live***

## Financial Health: Two Keys for Success (Live and Give)

**Purpose:** To suggest two critical (yet doable) actions that can put you on track for financial stability while you are working. They will also set you up to retire the way you want.

**The Discussion:** The first thing everyone can do that will enhance future financial security and success is *to decide* how they're going to live. This works at almost any salary level. [Though I must note that there are folks today who are not paid a living wage. Here, we must be mindful of that situation, and advocate for improvements while still working to help them formulate a budget or plan for spending.]

Here's how living decisively works. First, think about your finances and future. Many people procrastinate planning or saving. You must sit down and draw up a plan now. *Living and retiring well is not about math.* It's psychology and *how* we think about money. It's about discipline. We must learn to live *below* our financial means. That's a decision.

When you live on less than you make, you are automatically set up to survive a lower retirement income. For example, experts mention needing 70-80% of your pre-retirement income to live comfortably in retirement. Let's talk about how to make that work.

**Action: Live** (and pay attention to the details)

1. Write a spending plan (a.k.a., a budget).
2. Reduce eating out (which is the number one expense for many).
3. Check your subscriptions (cable, streaming services, magazines, music online, and your kids' expenses). These add up wildly.
4. Compare car and home insurance rates. Switch if you can get similar coverage at a better rate.

5. Do an Internet search for: "Biggest unnecessary expenses." (Think about your *wants vs. needs*.)
6. Do a "debt snowball" (See Dave Ramsey's approach of paying off your debt from smallest-to-largest).
7. Start a Roth IRA (now).

 Challenge to achieve financial freedom: Look at the seven items above.

> 1. Which could you begin doing now? Seriously. Today.
>
> 2. Which could you begin next week?
>
> 3. Imagine your life in five years: What does it look like if you have followed these concepts? How might you feel inside?

How much will you need in retirement? These questions will help you plan:

1. If you have a house/land, will it be paid off?
2. What are the ongoing taxes, insurance, and upkeep each year?
3. If you plan to rent, what's your ongoing monthly cost (with inflation)?
4. Are you the *new car type*?
5. Do you want to help kids/grandkids pay for college?
6. Do you want to travel?
7. Do you want to work part time?
8. Do you want to do volunteer work?

Challenge to achieve retirement freedom: Look at the eight items above.

1. Which is most important?

2. Which is not necessary, but perhaps a desired option?

3. Imagine your life in your retirement years: What does it look like if you have followed these concepts? How might you feel inside?

**For additional reading:** Ramsey, Dave. (2007). *The Total Money Makeover: A Proven Plan for Financial Fitness.* Nelson Books.

## General Reflections:

One thing that struck me about this topic was: _____
_____

I'm still pondering *(and may seek more information on)*: _____
_____

As a result of this reflection, I plan to: _____
_____
_____

# Conversation 25b - *Give*

## Financial Health: Two Keys for Success (Live and Give)

**The Discussion:** Again, living and retiring well is not about math. It's *how* we think about money. There is a tremendous amount of ancient wisdom on giving. In Judaism (the Mosaic Law), they stipulated a *tithe* which literally meant giving 10% of your wealth. In Christianity, Jesus extended the meaning of a tithe to make it less legalistic and more heartfelt. In Islam, the Zakat (alms giving) is one of the *Five Pillars*. In Sikhism, they encourage the Dasvandh (giving one tenth). And outside of religious tenets, non-religious and secular writings have wonderful ideas of *Giving What We Can* (GWWC) for altruistic associations in which members pledge at least 10% of their income to charities.

In *The Book of Joy*, His Holiness the Dalai Lama and Archbishop Desmond Tutu (with Doug Abrams) say, "It seems money can buy happiness, if we spend it on other people." They cite research that shows how generosity is one of the four fundamental brain circuits that track with long-term well-being.

 Giving questions:

1. How do you feel about giving?

2. Has it been a partial or consistent action / philosophy in your life? Why or why not?

**Action: Give** (to causes or needs of others). Giving changes your thinking. When you freely give away money or things or your time (with no strings attached) several things happen:

1. You help others (a cause, a person, etc.).
2. You focus on others and become less self-centric (which research shows is a positive path for joy and satisfaction in life).
3. You learn self-discipline. (Again, read the research on the benefits of this.)
4. You train your brain to recognize and remember your good fortune (e.g., of having a job). This increases internal gratitude and improves health according to research studies.

Here are some key questions:

 Challenge to achieve giving freedom: Look at the four items above.

1. Which sounds most important to you? Why?

2. If you could learn more about one of the items, which would it be? How might that help you?

**Summary:** We can train our brains on living and giving. When we tell ourselves we can live on 80% or 90%, we begin to change how we think and feel and act with money. The actions of living and giving can absolutely provide financial peace and security for our future.

**Homework:** Make a retirement bucket list. Whether you're twenty or forty or sixty years of age, make a list of what you want to retire *to*. That is, don't retire *from* something, but retire *to* something new. Then ponder how adopting *living and giving* now can make it happen.

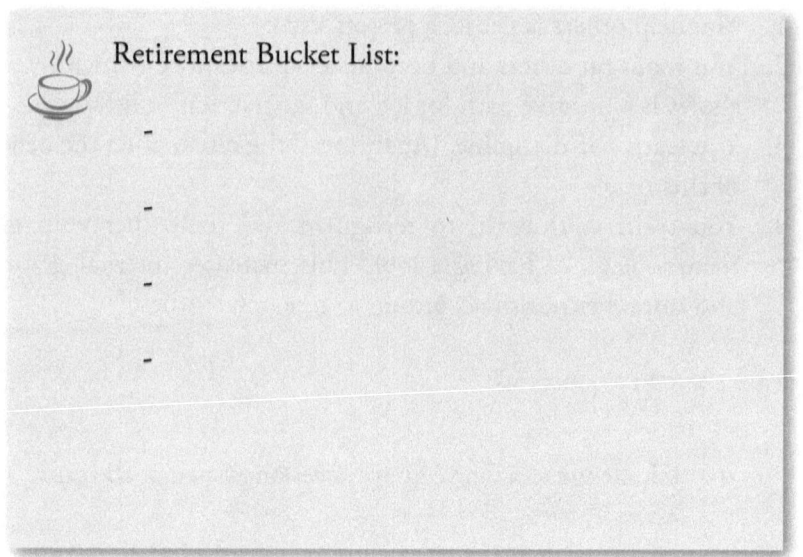

## General Reflections:

One thing that struck me about this topic was: _____
_____

I'm still pondering *(and may seek more information on)*: _____
_____

As a result of this reflection, I plan to: _____
_____
_____

# Conversations
# for Expanding
# Points of View

**Conversation 26**

### E+R=O (Event + Response = Outcome)

**Purpose:** To help you improve how you respond to any and all events that occur in day-to-day living.

Let's jump right into this one. Imagine someone is tailgating you. And I mean they are *right up on your bumper!* Think about what you do at that moment.

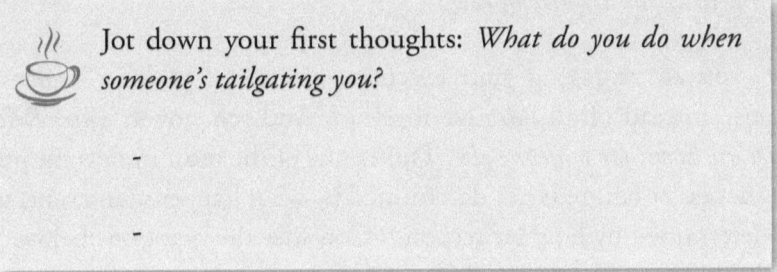

We all have options. Right? Do you tap the brake pedal? Do you try to move out of their way? Or do you wave at them (with one finger)?

> **My alleged tailgating incident:**
>
> In the summer of 2016, I was apparently driving a bit too close to the person in front of me. When he *finally* put on his blinker to turn right, halfway through the turn he hit the brakes. I had to swerve to miss rear-ending his car. What nerve! At that moment, I really wanted to lay on the horn, but I remembered my fifteen-year-old daughter was sitting in the passenger seat. We were going to our church parking lot where I was to bestow good driving lessons. At that very moment, this formula popped into my head: $E+R=O$.

What does E+R=O mean?

In 2004, author Jack Canfield outlined this formula to help people improve how they respond to any event that occurs in day-to-day living. **E+R=O (event + response = outcome)**

Events happen all day every day. We take great notice of those that are unexpected or stressors. The key is to change your gut reaction to a thoughtful response. In this manner, you are much more likely to achieve the desired outcome. But *how* do you do it?

Believe it or not, it's simple. First: *Press pause*. Then, ask yourself: *What does this situation require of me?*

Here, you are engaging your executive-brain and making a measured response instead of an emotive reaction. And remember: *Your Response creates an Event for someone else.* This is one of the most important points. Our success or failure is not determined by what happens (an event) to us. It is determined by how we respond. Consider the questions below. Jot a few things that come to mind.

How might you *respond* the next time someone really irritates you?

What difference might your thoughtful response make, versus a gut reaction?

**Challenge:** Practice thinking about E+R=O for the next 24-hours. Look at everything as an *event*. Then, when the formula is in your brain, watch for an irritating *event*. Check yourself on how you respond. Pressing pause takes a lot of practice. Are you willing to give it a try? This can be a game-changer at both home and work.

**For additional reading:** Canfield, Jack (2004). The Success Principles. New York: Harper Collins.

## General Reflections:

One thing that struck me about this topic was: _____

_____

I'm still pondering *(and may seek more information on)*: _____

_____

As a result of this reflection, I plan to: _____

_____

_____

# Conversation 27

## Circle of Control: *Shift Your Focus. Reduce Worry.*

**Purpose:** To explain the simple concept of focusing on items within our circles of concern and control to direct our actions and reduce worry.

In Stephen Covey's book, *The 7 Habits of Highly Effective People,* he outlined the idea of a *circle of control* in which we might segregate difficult situations into three levels (or circles):

The **Circle of Concern** includes things we often worry about and likely *should* be concerned with but cannot control. Examples include the weather and the economy.

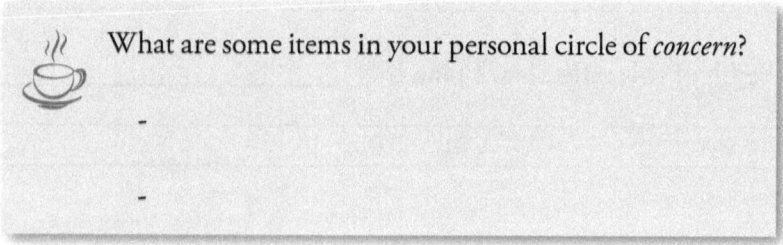

What are some items in your personal circle of *concern*?

The **Circle of Influence** includes areas where we can have some choice, action, or impact. Examples include our health and a job interview. i.e., With some preparation, we can influence the outcomes of these things.

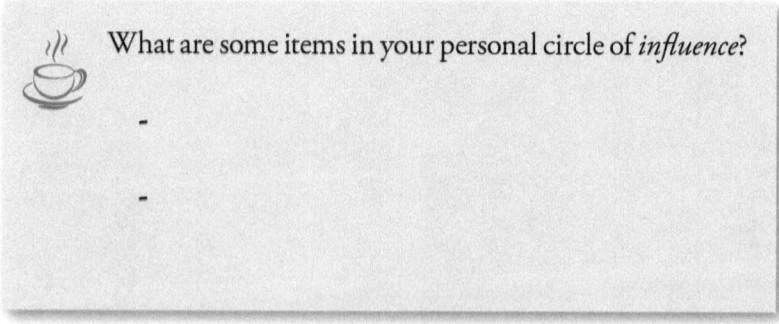

What are some items in your personal circle of *influence*?

The **Circle of Control** is the one we all love. This innermost circle consists of all the things we can take action on. Some examples might include how much we spend on eating out, whether we exercise, or fasten our seat belts.

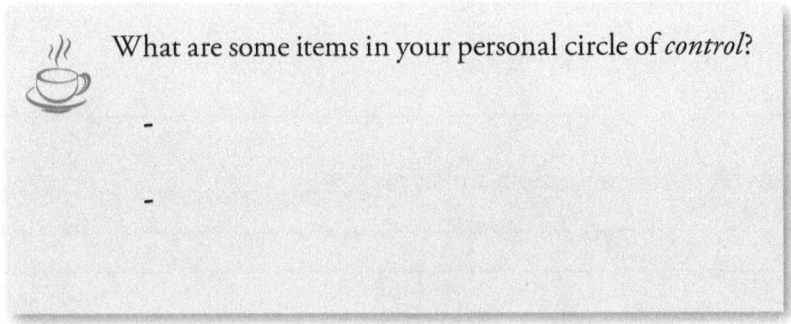

What are some items in your personal circle of *control*?

**The Discussion:** We love it when we can control things. We love to take action and make things happen. But in the Circle of Concern, we must remember that we have little-to-no ability for control. Concern is legitimate. But try not to expend your energies there. If we can shift our mindset to think about what we can influence and control, we can use our energy more wisely, and likely be much more effective. We also increase our resilience, productivity, and success.

Here's a final challenge question:

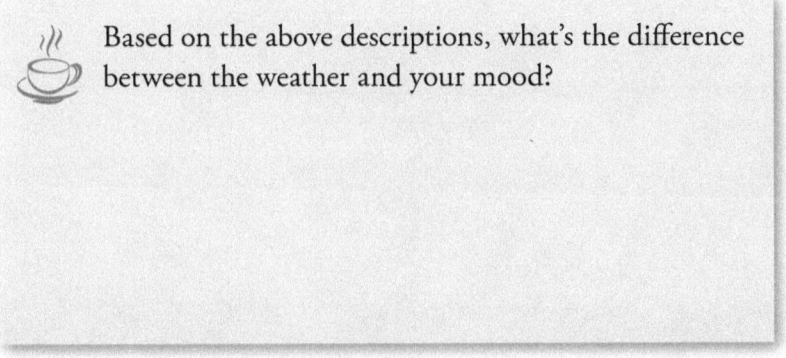

Based on the above descriptions, what's the difference between the weather and your mood?

I love asking this question. I'm sure you can immediately see where I'm going with it. No one can control whether it rains or snows, but we all can decide how it affects us. That decision is within our Circle of Control.

## General Reflections:

One thing that struck me about this topic was: _____
_____

I'm still pondering *(and may seek more information on)*: _____
_____

As a result of this reflection, I plan to: _____
_____
_____

**Conversation 28**

## Hidden Diversity

**Purpose:** This is a reminder that most aspects of diversity are not outwardly visible, but recognizing hidden variables can be of great value to your personal and professional life. Let's jump in.

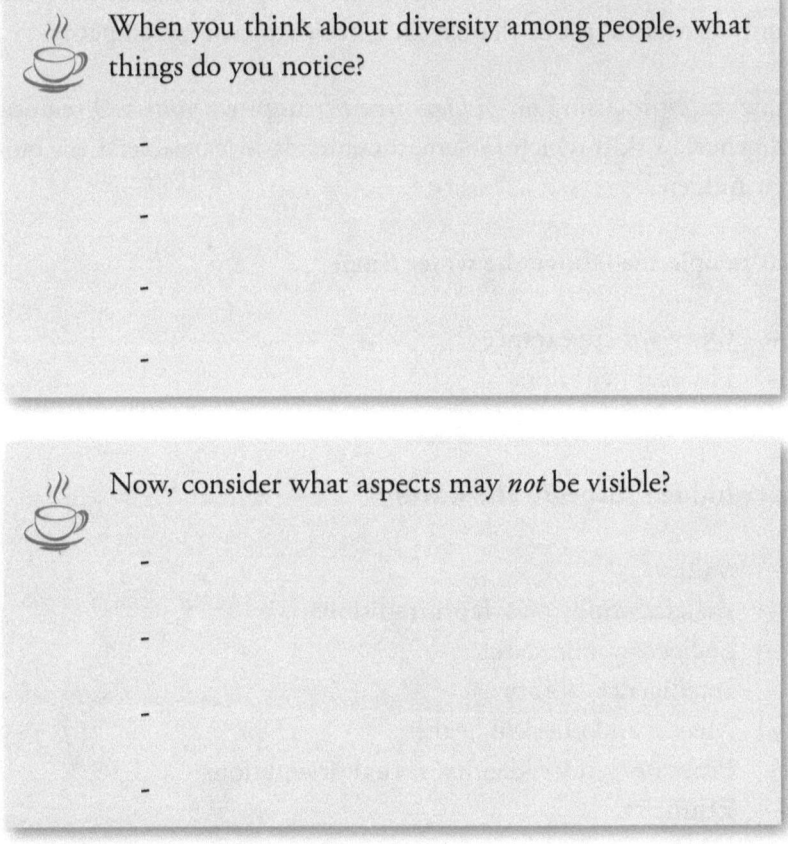

When you think about diversity among people, what things do you notice?

-

-

-

Now, consider what aspects may *not* be visible?

-

-

-

**The Discussion:** I regularly meet new people, and I talk daily with people I've known for years. But how well do I really know them? How well do they really know me? Aside from a couple of friends in the counselor and clergy professions, I know few who can set aside their first visual impression (or their one-hundredth time seeing someone), truly look beneath the surface, and remind themselves that this person may have sadness or joy of which I know nothing. They may have recently experienced loss or gain, an acute mental health crisis, an ongoing battle with dyslexia, addiction, food insecurity, or any number of other afflictions (or prosperity). We may observe signs, but we simply do not know.

If we do not pause and remind ourselves of these hidden differences, it is easy to interact on the surface in an "I - It" transaction. In *Social Intelligence*, Daniel Goleman describes this as treating others as objects, not persons. The inverse is the "I - You" relationship in which others' feelings not only matter to us but change us. This is a picture of empathy.

So how might focusing on *hidden diversity* improve your EQ (emotional intelligence), a skill which Goleman contends is learnable? Let's quickly review hidden aspects of diversity.

**What people see (above the water line):**

- Outward appearance
- Physical behaviors
- Sound of voice (including accents)

**What's hidden (beneath the waves):**

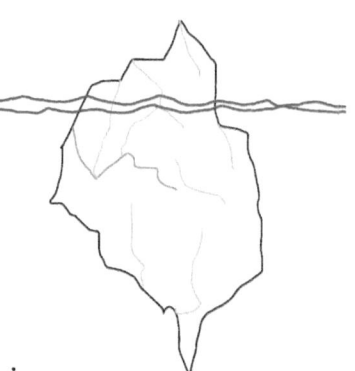

- Values
- Beliefs, worldviews, faith traditions
- Socioeconomic status
- Intelligence, ability
- Mental and physical health
- Pronoun/gender identity, sexual orientations
- Ethnicity
- DNA / physical variation
- History, geography, and more

I love that last point with history and geography. We sometimes miss these aspects. For example, I am fully Appalachian—a geographic, socioeconomic, and cultural designation. But people do not *see* that outwardly, nor do they *hear* much of an accent when I speak. But my family holds close this proud heritage. We celebrate our unique foods and music and family and faiths. We also experience stereotyping and degrading humor. Raising awareness of hidden diversity can help everyone become more sensitive and considerate of others. It can also strengthen friendships and teams at work, quickening goal attainment.

Here is a closing question to consider for more personal reflection.

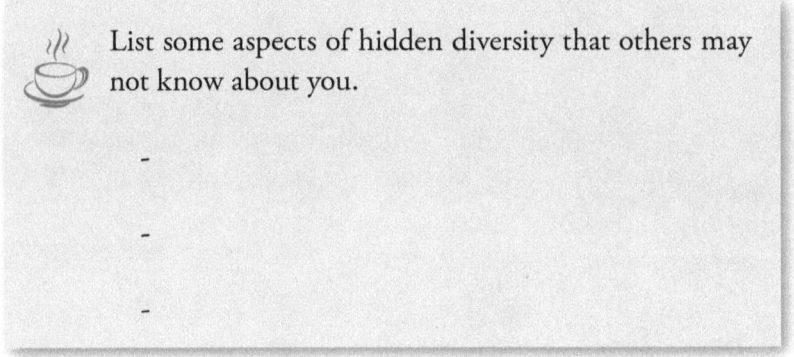

List some aspects of hidden diversity that others may not know about you.

-

-

-

**Homework:** This week, casually observe someone with whom you interact and wish to know better or improve the relationship. Become curious about hidden diversity, and initiate a conversation. Think about how learning more about others can help you improve your leadership skills.

## General Reflections:

One thing that struck me about this topic was: _____

_____

I'm still pondering *(and may seek more information on)*: _____

_____

As a result of this reflection, I plan to: _____

_____

_____

## Conversation 29

### Seek Diverse Relationships

**Purpose:** To consider the benefits of having diverse relationships. To increase our thinking on how aspects of diversity and inclusiveness can help broaden our perspectives, discover solutions, and energize creativity.

Here's a simple but critical question:

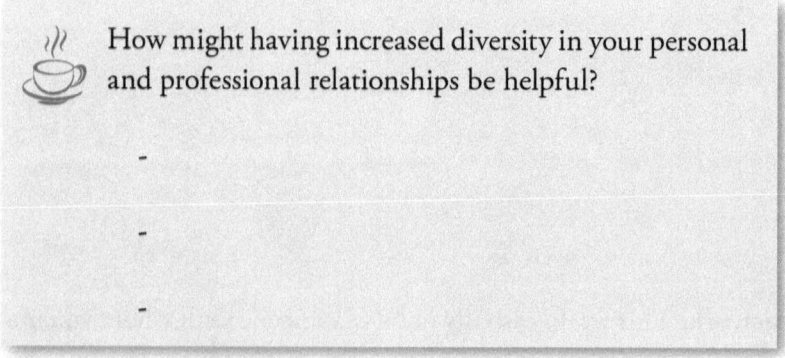

How might having increased diversity in your personal and professional relationships be helpful?

Explore your thinking here. Do you presently have many relationships with people who differ from yourself? Here are some prompting questions that might help:

1. What might you learn from a person twenty years younger than you?
2. What wisdom might you share with someone ten years older?
3. Are you comfortable with friends or coworkers who have different skin colors?
4. Do you have friends or colleagues with language barriers?
5. Would you be comfortable with someone who dressed differently (e.g. wore religious-based clothing)?
6. What if they had a different sexual orientation or gender identity?
7. Would you be comfortable working with someone who may be on the autistic spectrum?

8. How might working with someone from a different socio-economic class feel?
9. What if someone looked the same as you outwardly, but you think or feel you have nothing in common?
10. Is it possible to connect with someone in a meaningful way even though they may be different?

**The Discussion:** We don't always stop to think about diversity or inclusion in our day-to-day work and life. But deliberately thinking about these things can benefit all involved. Diversity adds richness to planning, problem solving, and strategic communication. Diversity expands perspective, a critical component of navigating the varying pathways to mission attainment. Diversity energizes creativity and improves organizational culture. With open, honest, and authentic engagement, you can more quickly build trust.

Challenge question: Look at the ten items above.

1. Which two or three stand out in your mind?
   -
   -
   -

2. What might you want to learn about the items you listed above?
   -
   -
   -

3. How might expanding your diverse relationships benefit you and your work (or volunteer) organization?
   -
   -
   -

**Homework:** Choose one of the ten items above where you would like to grow. Do some reading. Reach out and connect with someone who could help you.

## General Reflections:

One thing that struck me about this topic was: _____
_____

I'm still pondering *(and may seek more information on)*: _____
_____

As a result of this reflection, I plan to: _____
_____
_____

# Conversation 30

## Building Your Emotional Intelligence (EQ)

**Purpose:** To help you understand the construct of emotional intelligence, and how to increase it to help your career and life.

**Background:** We often hear people dismissing social or emotional skills as *touchy-feely*. Many still use the term *soft skills*. Over the past dozen years, my interactions with employers (from manufacturing to government, service, education, and tech) summarily state that they can teach someone the job, but "we need people who can communicate and work as a team." The business, industry, service, and knowledge sectors of our economy are demanding these *critical skills*. EQ is the critical skill of the future.

**Emotional Intelligence (EI) (EQ)** – This was defined by Daniel Goleman in 1995. I think of these ideas as other ways *to be smart*. In brief, EQ considers:

- how one recognizes their own and other's emotions
- how one discriminates different feelings
- how one uses emotional information to guide thinking and behavior

If you understand your feelings, you may use them to:

- Better connect with your family, coworkers, and community.
- Make better decisions; motivate yourself and others.
- Find empathy; be positive; encourage hope.
- Improve interactions; manage business, professional, student, familial, and personal relationships.

**Activity:** Below is an outline of Goleman's five *Personal and Social Competencies* of EQ. Take a few minutes and consider each, noting where you might like to learn more and/or grow personally.

1. Self-Awareness – You know your strengths, preferences, resources, intuitions, as well as your limitations. You know what Simon Sinek describes as your *why*.

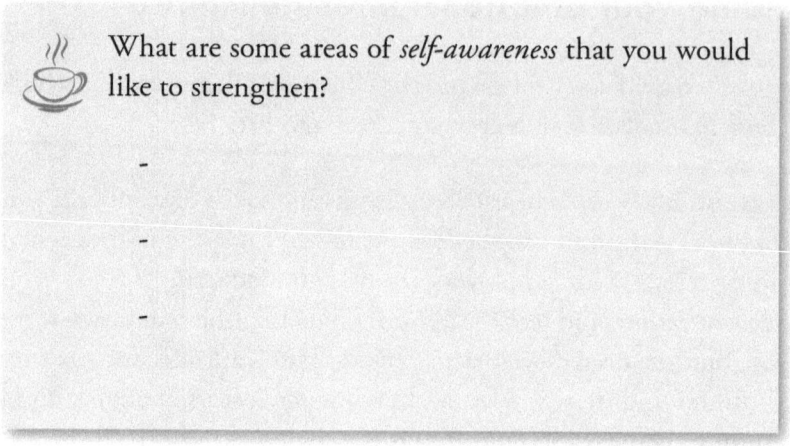

What are some areas of *self-awareness* that you would like to strengthen?

-

-

-

2. Self-Regulation – You control and channel events, moods, impulses, and resources.

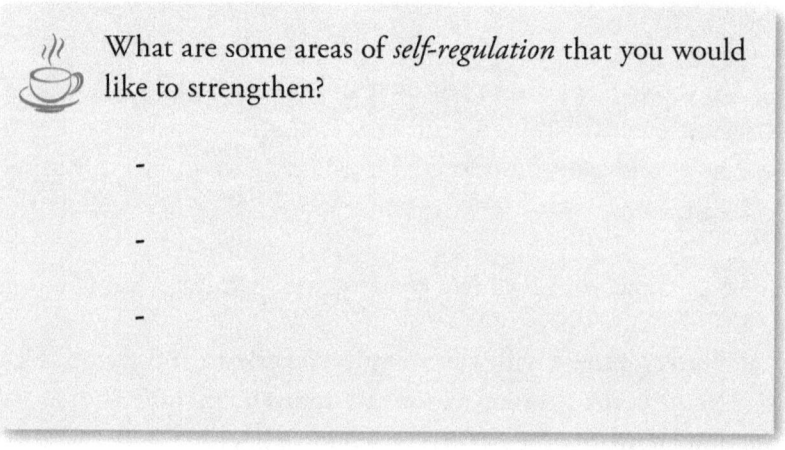

What are some areas of *self-regulation* that you would like to strengthen?

-

-

-

3. Motivation – You are driven to achieve beyond expectations. Your emotional tendencies guide or facilitate reaching goals.

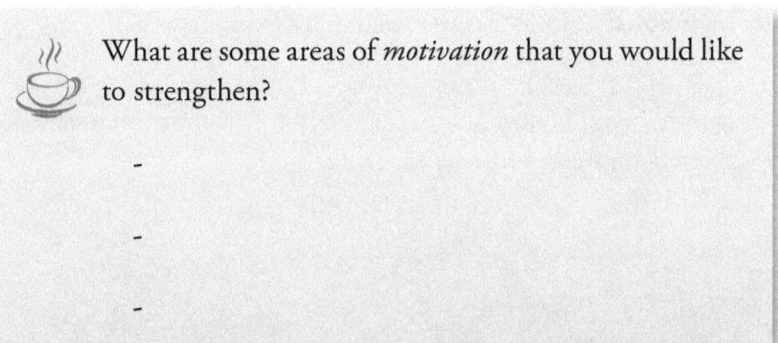

What are some areas of *motivation* that you would like to strengthen?

-

-

-

4. Empathy (Social Awareness) – You are aware of feelings, needs, concerns of others. You thoughtfully consider other's feelings in the process of making intelligent decisions. This is highly needed to do teamwork well.

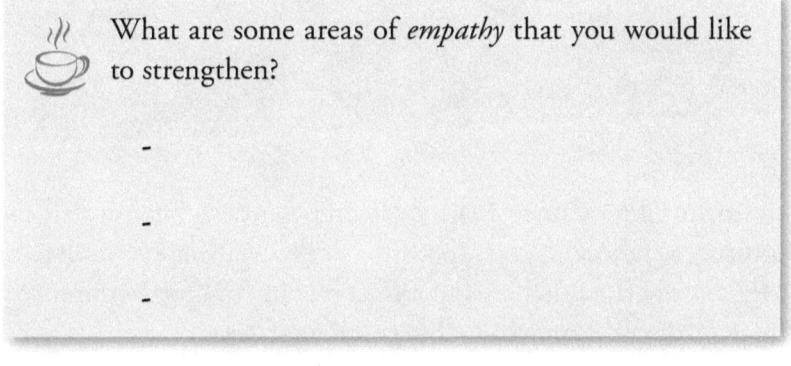

What are some areas of *empathy* that you would like to strengthen?

-

-

-

5. Social Skills – You are adept at managing relationships with others and inducing desirable responses.

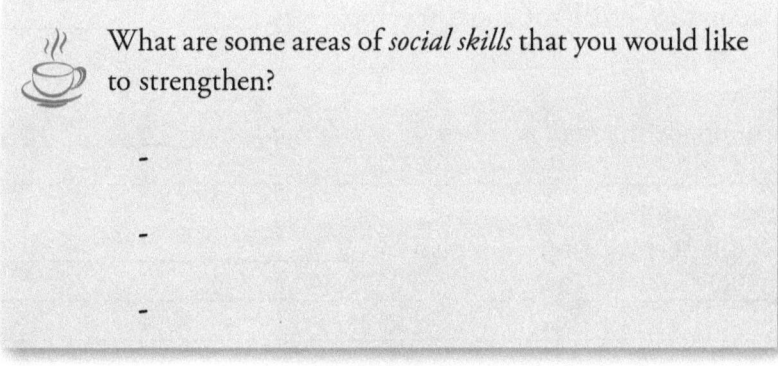

What are some areas of *social skills* that you would like to strengthen?

-

-

-

**Bonus questions:** Consider these final questions.

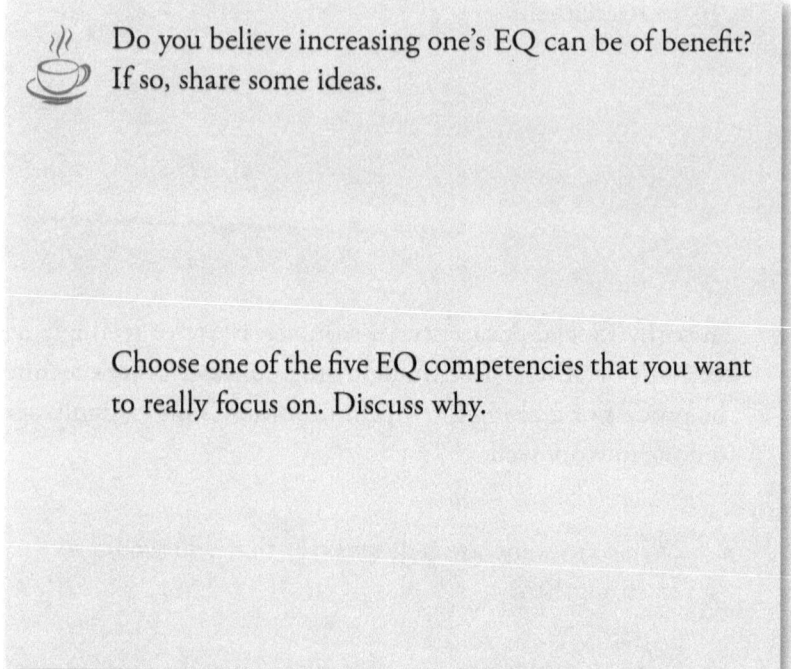

Do you believe increasing one's EQ can be of benefit? If so, share some ideas.

Choose one of the five EQ competencies that you want to really focus on. Discuss why.

**Homework:** Choose one of the five competencies. Then watch for an opportunity to reflect on that aspect this week. Challenge yourself to make a mental note of the situation and reflect on how you might improve your interactions the next time something similar arises.

## General Reflections:

One thing that struck me about this topic was: _____
_____

I'm still pondering *(and may seek more information on)*: _____
_____

As a result of this reflection, I plan to: _____
_____
_____

**Conversation 31**

## Building Your Social Intelligence

**Purpose:** To help you understand the construct of social intelligence and grow your skills to help your career and life.

**Background:** About ten years after publishing his seminal work on emotional intelligence, Daniel Goleman dove even deeper into our brains by examining research on the chemistry and connections that drive us. These, subsequently, allow our societies, workplaces, and families to function and thrive.

In brief, *social intelligence* is a construct that considers our ability to accurately read other people around us, as well as understand the context, and then (the key) act appropriately. That's pretty basic stuff. Goleman goes on to claim that the *way we engage* with our social environment has profound consequences for our external success. Herein, we need to pay attention.

>  Why might *paying attention* to our social environment matter so much as we seek career success? List two or three ideas.
>
> -
>
> -
>
> -

One of the key concepts is to consider how we view ourselves. Goleman notes "self-absorption in all its forms kills empathy." If we are focused on self, our world contracts and *our* problems are all that matter. If we can instead shift our focus to others, our world expands. This mental health benefit has now been measured physiologically. Focusing on others allows our problems to drift to the periphery (and thus seem smaller). This increases our capacity for connection and meaningful action.

**The Discussion:** From a personal and professional development standpoint, Goleman says social intelligence is the sweet spot for achievement. He says there are times when we may become *frazzled*, and our emotional upsurges hamper the effective working of our brain's executive center. This immediately "handicaps our abilities for learning, for holding information, for reacting flexibly, for creativity, for planning and organizing." These moments can push us into cognitive dysfunction. We are distracted by thoughts that hijack our attention and "squeeze our cognitive resources."

Here's a question to ponder:

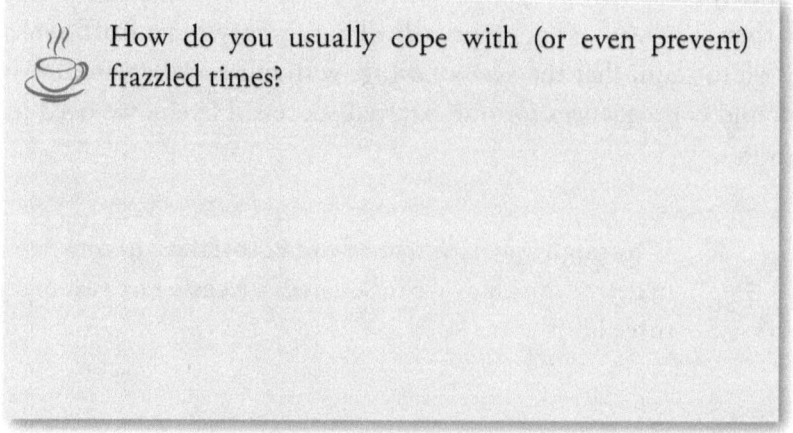

How do you usually cope with (or even prevent) frazzled times?

Reflect on the *E+R=O* formula. If you remember, when we are able to press pause and control our *response* (instead of *reacting*), we achieve a better *outcome*. It works. Social intelligence is a lot about pressing pause.

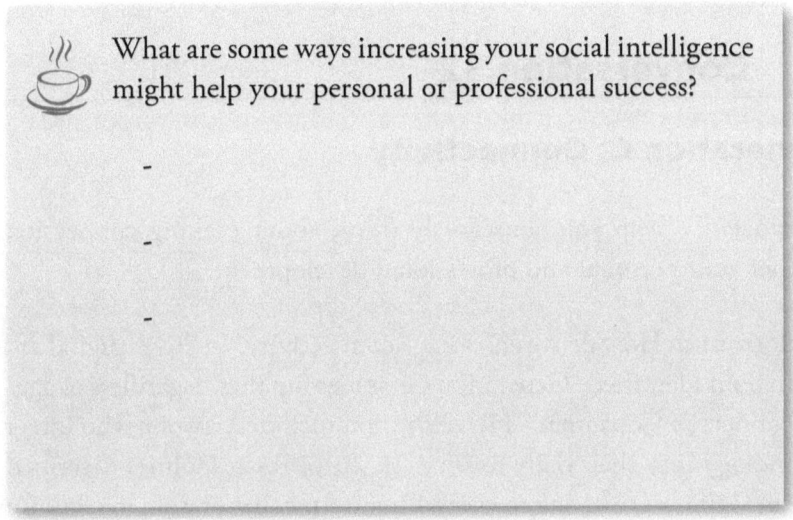

What are some ways increasing your social intelligence might help your personal or professional success?

- 
- 
- 

**For additional reading:** Goleman, Daniel (2006). *Social Intelligence: The New Science of Human Relationships.*

## General Reflections:

One thing that struck me about this topic was: _____

I'm still pondering *(and may seek more information on)*: _____

As a result of this reflection, I plan to: _____

**Conversation 32**

## Generation C: Connectivity

**Purpose:** To help you consciously think about making connections to further your personal and professional development.

**Background:** How do we encourage connectivity? In 2012, digital analyst Brian Solis identified "Generation C" as a group that, regardless of age, was a "Connected Consumer." His definition included anyone who integrates technology into their daily routine. In 2016, Ryan Holmes described the "C" in Gen C as referring to everything from collaboration to community, computerization, and content. He emphasized that the key point was connectivity.

This is nothing new. In the 1980s, we called it *networking*. Today, there is the additional, necessary element of using electronic devices to aid and enhance these connections. The idea remains the same. By encouraging the habit of connectivity, we can see more doors opened and discover opportunities otherwise missed. When thinking about making connections, three questions can help. Take a moment to jot down a few thoughts.

1. What am I trying to accomplish? _____

2. Who can help me? _____

3. How can I contribute to them to deepen our relationship? _____
   _____

Question #3 helps us think about what John Stepper, author of *Working Out Loud*, says is the key to connectivity. That is, instead of connecting to *get something*, we should lead with *generosity*, "investing in relationships that give you access to other people, knowledge, and possibilities." The generosity component is critical.

Reflection question:

 Where might you make a new connection in which you share your talent, genuinely seeking to help further a cause, but that might also result in a career advancement?

-

-

-

**Summary:** Connectivity is key. But do not wait for the *perfect* opportunity to reach out. In *The Fred Factor*, Mark Sanborn smartly advises us to simply take opportunities, and then make them as perfect as we can. Take action. Get connected. Create your own luck.

**For additional reading:** Holmes, Ryan (October 12, 2016). *Inc Magazine* - http://www.inc.com/ryan-holmes/move-over-millennials-5-things-you-need-to-know-about-generation-c.html

Sanborn, Mark (2004). *The Fred factor: How passion in your work and life can turn the ordinary into the extraordinary* (1st Currency ed.). Currency/Doubleday.

Stepper, John (2015). *Working Out Loud for a Better Career and Life*. New York: Ikigai Press.

## General Reflections:

One thing that struck me about this topic was: _____
_____

I'm still pondering *(and may seek more information on)*: _____
_____

As a result of this reflection, I plan to: _____
_____
_____

**Conversation 33**

## Spirituality & Faith Traditions

**Purpose:** This conversation asks us to consider a topic some find difficult or even inappropriate for work, but which may challenge us to introspection. It also aims to potentially increase acknowledgement of (and even honor for) diverse traditions among those with whom we live and work.

Introductory question:

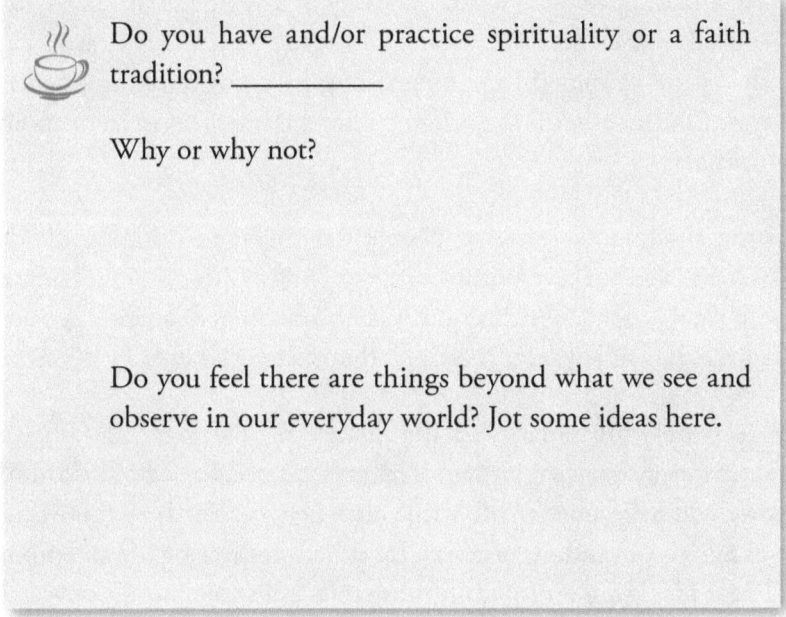

Do you have and/or practice spirituality or a faith tradition? _____

Why or why not?

Do you feel there are things beyond what we see and observe in our everyday world? Jot some ideas here.

**Background:** Psychologists, medical doctors, leadership researchers, wisdom writers, philosophers, rabis, pastors, imams, gurus, and others have long observed that people inherently yearn for a purpose-driven life. We want to do or serve something beyond our personal goals and economic self-interest. We want to be remembered for doing something good during our lifetime. For many, faith traditions help fill this void.

Multiple research studies have shown positive mental and physical health benefits for people who practice some sort of faith tradition. In a 2012 comprehensive review of hundreds of studies, Koenig found research clearly shows people with more religion and/or spirituality have better physical and mental health and recover more quickly from health problems. Other studies from Azar and Sweeney have linked adults' religious involvement to better health and well-being outcomes, including lower risk of premature death.

In addition, various faith traditions bring beautiful diversity to our workplaces. They are part of the tenets of diversity, equity, and inclusion.

**Discussion:** What does it mean to have faith in a spiritual sense? Some people see faith or religion as another way of knowing, empirically tested and verified by the observable fruits of love and action. There are changed lives that attest to something unseen. These are powerful arguments and evidence. On the other hand, some contend there is no need or room for the spiritual.

With the thought of bringing people together and bridging divides, I undertook a study of seventeenth century philosopher and mathematician Blaise Pascal. In his posthumously published manuscript, *Pensées*, he posited the idea of a wager, "betting" that there is a God.

A lot of people misunderstand the nuance of his wager idea. In short, Pascal reasoned that even if there is no creator or God, if we live as if there were, we will have a better life while alive here on Earth by following the general moral conventions of caring for others, respecting life and property, etc. These ideals are repeated in numerous belief systems. Conversely, if God is truly real, we need not fear death. We gain some sort of life for eternity when we trust therein.

Here's the disconnect: Most people focus on the wager—the bet—thinking Pascal is hedging. In doing so, we completely miss his actual thesis: *We don't have to wait till we die to win the bet.* We can have life and love and completeness now, essentially creating our own paradise here on Earth while we are physically alive. It's a fascinating idea. In early 1971,

John Lennon essentially intoned this same general concept when he sang, "Imagine all the people, living life in peace."

Please take a few minutes to think about these questions:

 How might learning about (and acknowledging) various faith traditions enrich your workplace?

Whether you have a strong faith tradition, or none, could you be open to discussing topics (such as the purpose of life) that are very meaningful to many? How might these discussions strengthen your work culture and objectives?

**Summary questions for pondering:** Regardless of your faith tradition, spiritual practice, or contentment with not needing a religious construct, could Pascal's notion of practicing kindness and love and care for others in this world pay benefits (personally and societally) now? If we become more respectful of deep convictions held by others, especially when they are different from ours, might we improve our work culture and outcomes?

**Challenge:** Look back at your response to the introductory question in this conversation. What might you do to investigate your existing personal beliefs more deeply, or to learn more about those of others to further your understanding? How might that enhance your working or personal relationships?

## References:

Azar, B. (2010). A reason to believe. *APA Monitor on Psychology.* Vol 41, No. 11. Available at: https://www.apa.org/monitor/2010/12/believe

Koenig HG. Religion, spirituality, and health: the research and clinical implications. ISRN Psychiatry. 2012 Dec 16;2012:278730. doi: 10.5402/2012/278730. PMID: 23762764; PMCID: PMC3671693.

Sweeney, C. (2018). Religious upbringing linked to better health and well-being during early adulthood. Harvard University, School of Public Health. Available at: https://www.hsph.harvard.edu/news/press-releases/religious-upbringing-adult-health/

## General Reflections:

One thing that struck me about this topic was: _____

_____

I'm still pondering *(and may seek more information on)*: _____

_____

As a result of this reflection, I plan to: _____

_____

_____

**Conversation 34**

## Changing Perspective: *Embracing the Art of Possibility*

**Purpose:** To help you remember to consider the limits of your own, internal, inherent perspective when faced with an issue, or when trying to add diversity and generate ideas.

**Background:** We all know our perspective can be biased. In fact, it is. We naturally see things from our point of view which is, of course, limited. One of the easiest things that will expand *possibility* (as well as options, solutions, creativity, etc.) is to simply change or broaden our perspective. But how do we do that?

Consider this question.

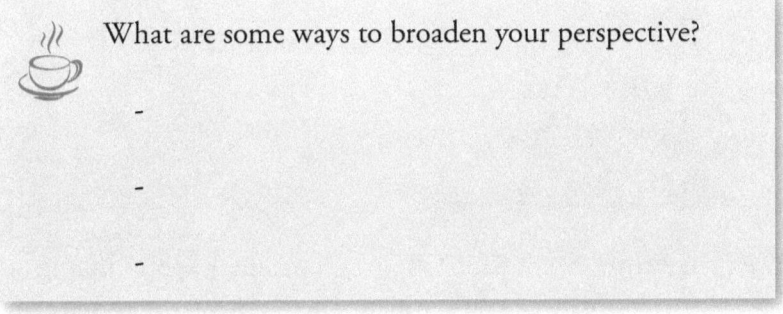

**The Discussion:** How does one expand their perspective? We learned with E+R=O that when an event happens, we need to press pause and engage our executive brain (responding versus reacting). While that executive brain is engaged, we need to become aware or simply remind ourselves that we're seeing whatever event only from *our* perspective.

At this point of awareness, we must pause and ponder some key questions. Imagine a scenario in which you are faced with a challenge. Perhaps someone vehemently disagrees with you. Ask yourself this:

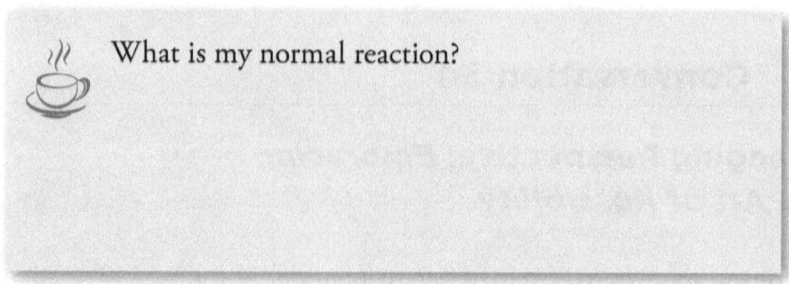

What is my normal reaction?

Then consider this: What assumption(s) am I making that I may not be aware I'm making? These may be about the person who's disagreeing with me, or something else. These limit options, potential solutions, creativity, and possibility.

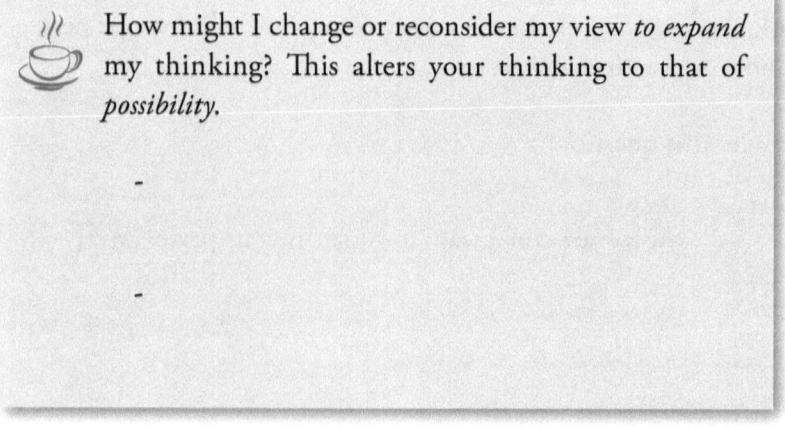

How might I change or reconsider my view *to expand* my thinking? This alters your thinking to that of *possibility*.

In *The Fred Factor*, Mark Sanborn gives a business application in which he says *perspective* can catapult you to the front of the market. When working to create value for others, Sanborn says you can "replace money with imagination" and outthink the competition versus outspending them. One way to accomplish this is by consciously changing your perspective. This will expand possibilities.

Here are some other practical ways to expand your perspective. The next time you're faced with a problem or a narrow view of a situation, asking yourself these questions can help.

If I were someone else (who, perhaps, had different knowledge of the situation), how might I view this? [Consider how you could bring this question to mind when it's needed.]

-

-

-

 What might a friend (or a wise grandparent, counselor, clergy, etc.) suggest in this situation? [Here is another *pure perspective* question. Jot down the name of a person or two who you'd ask for advice or perspective.]

-

-

-

**Summary:** If we can remember to press pause (E+R=O), engage our executive brain, and ask ourselves the perspective questions when faced with an event, we stand to expand possibilities and positive outcomes.

**Additional Reading:** Sanborn, Mark (2004). *The Fred factor: How passion in your work and life can turn the ordinary into the extraordinary* (1st Currency ed.). Currency/Doubleday.

## General Reflections:

One thing that struck me about this topic was: _____
_____

I'm still pondering *(and may seek more information on):* _____
_____

As a result of this reflection, I plan to: _____
_____
_____

# Anytime Conversation Prompts

**Conversation 35**

## Perspective Shifting

**Purpose:** To consider *perspective* more deeply and challenge yourself to consciously employ perspective shifting *on a daily basis.*

**Background:** In prior conversations, we have talked about *changing* your perspective. Now it's time to go deeper and truly challenge yourself. *Shifting* perspective can be one of the most powerful devices in anyone's personal or professional tool kit. True perspective shifting opens our eyes to more diverse, unique, and creative solutions to problems. It unlocks doors and identifies sometimes hidden possibility. Again, this works both personally and professionally.

Below are three questions designed to help you think about shifting your perspective. But first, try this brief kinesthetic experiment. I learned it from my OSU colleague, Steve Brady, nearly twenty years ago.

> Stand if you are able. (Seriously. Do this. Standing or moving provides an immediate perspective change.) Now, fold your hands, interlocking fingers. Look down at your hands. Which thumb is on top? (Some will find their right, others the left.)
>
> Now unfold your hands and refold them, this time *with your other thumb on top.* It feels a bit weird, doesn't it?
>
> Okay. Now, fold your arms in front of your chest. You have done this a million times. It's natural. Look down. Which arm is on top? (Again, some will find their right, others the left.)
>
> Now for the challenge: Try *folding your arms the other way* with the "wrong" arm on top. You may have to focus to find success. For most people, this feels very awkward.

[Pro tip: Use this as an opening experiment with a group who is trying to solve a problem or make an important decision. It awakens brain cells and can remind people that there are *other ways* of doing things. It's also quite funny to watch.]

What does this perspective shifting really mean? We are creatures of habit. Our brains are conditioned to our personal reality, our own singular-sighted perspective. So how can we get out of our comfort zone and discover a different way of thinking, a new approach that might move us more quickly toward our goal? Like crossing our arms the "wrong" way, it might be uncomfortable at first. But when we challenge ourselves to be open to new, more diverse ideas and ways of thinking, new possibilities arise.

Use the questions below as an exercise to try to change or expand your perspective. Think of a problem you are facing, or a difficult decision you need to make.

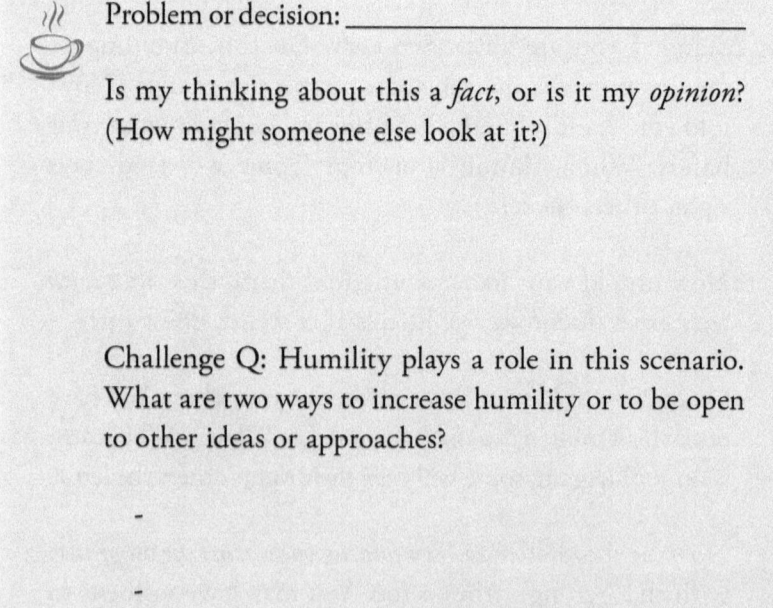

Problem or decision: _____

Is my thinking about this a *fact*, or is it my *opinion*? (How might someone else look at it?)




Challenge Q: Humility plays a role in this scenario. What are two ways to increase humility or to be open to other ideas or approaches?

-

-

Problem or decision: _____

If I could be five years in the future looking back at this issue, what might I see?

Challenge Q: Projecting your vision into the future is pure perspective. Do you think you could deploy this approach during a stressful event? Describe how you might do that.

 Problem or decision: _____

Am I noticing the storyline in my own mind around this issue? (Could you shift the narrative or your interpretation to open new possibilities?) Jot down a few ideas on how you might do that.

**Summary:** Perspective shifting is a powerful tool. But it takes practice. Like E+R=O, you can know about it and that it is effective. But it can take a lifetime to master. That's okay. The best time to start is now.

## General Reflections:

One thing that struck me about this topic was: _____
_____

I'm still pondering *(and may seek more information on)*: _____
_____

As a result of this reflection, I plan to: _____
_____
_____

**Conversation 36**

## The Charles Schulz Challenge: Embracing Contentment

**Purpose:** To help you remember that some things, people, and places are more meaningful than others. This conversation aims to help you refocus on what matters, find contentment, and inspire you.

**The Discussion:** Have you been feeling successful lately? Or not so much? Are you accomplishing everything you want in your job? Are you getting those promotions and raises? Or do you wish you made a little more money? Do you wish you had more recognition?

In today's world, it's easy to get off track or focus on things that lead to dissatisfaction. This can sneak up on us. We often don't even notice it has happened. We see others who appear more wealthy, healthy, or successful, and our personal contentment with life drops. Is there a way to refocus?

A number of years ago, a short exercise that challenged people to refocus on the important parts of life circulated widely via social media. Many attributed it to Charles Schulz, the creator of the Peanuts comic strip. Whether he said it or only inspired it, Schulz often included philosophy into his work and brilliantly challenged astute readers to peer beyond the cartoon characters and think deeply about life.

Here is my version of the quiz. Please try it.

Jot down one or two responses for each question.

1. Name one or two of the wealthiest people in the world.

2. Name the last couple of Heisman trophy winners.

3. Name the last couple of Academy Award winners.

4. Name the last couple years of World Series or Super Bowl winners.

How did you do? Most folks have difficulty in answering all those questions. The headlines of yesterday fade quickly. Even big achievements by famous people are soon forgotten. Money and recognition do not lead to being contented in life.

With this in mind, here is a different challenge to work through.

Supply one or two responses to these questions.

1. List one or two teachers who made a positive impact on you.

2. Name a friend who helped you through a difficult time.

3. Name two people who taught you something worthwhile.

4. Think of a few people who have made you feel appreciated and special.

5. Think of three people you enjoy spending time with.

How did you do on this one? Was it easier?

The lesson is clear: The people who have influence in our lives should be the ones who care about us and invest time in things that matter: *Being a friend. Teaching. Giving encouragement. Sharing joy.* These are the things that lead to becoming more gratified with our lives. Comparing ourselves to the rich and recognized—including perhaps our neighbors with a bigger house or newer car—leads only to discontentment.

**The Key:** When we shift our focus to things that matter and invest in other people, it is recognized. That's the kind of recognition that matters. The authentic, caring person who focuses on what matters is practicing great leadership. This will be noticed. This is the kind of thing that can result in advancement in your workplace. But even if that advancement takes time, being a friendly coworker pays immediate dividends.

**Summary:** The next time you are feeling down or if you're feeling you're not accomplishing very much by the world's standards, refocus and remember this second list. Then, *go out and become one of these people on someone else's list.*

**Challenge:** Whose list might you like to land on? i.e., Who might you want to inspire or encourage? Send that person (or people) a note of encouragement today.

## General Reflections:

One thing that struck me about this topic was: _____
_____

I'm still pondering *(and may seek more information on)*: _____
_____

As a result of this reflection, I plan to: _____
_____
_____

**Conversation 37**

## Building Trust

**Purpose:** To help you understand and grow trust.

Consider this:

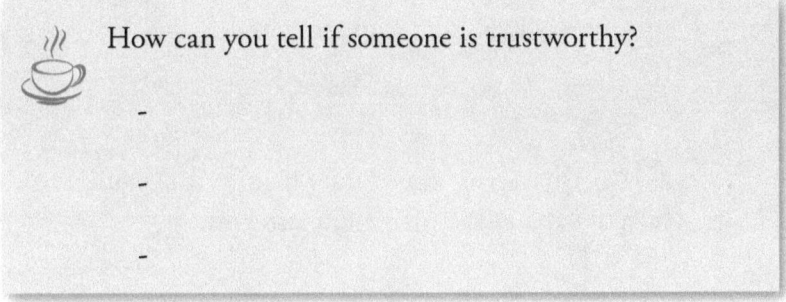

How can you tell if someone is trustworthy?

**The Discussion:** Whether we recognize this or not, when we encounter people at work, in social situations, or even within our own family, we are being evaluated as to how much others can trust us. It is not always a conscious, top of mind thought. But assuredly, our interactions are improved or impoverished based on how others perceive our trustworthiness.

Consider this:

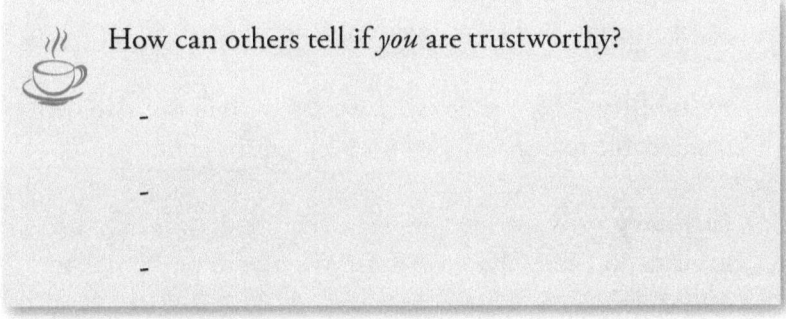

How can others tell if *you* are trustworthy?

Consultant and visual storyteller Tanmay Vora says, "Trust is not something you demand, it is something you have to earn." The way to earn trust is by having clear intentions, taking action that supports those intentions, and, most importantly, acting with the utmost integrity through human connection. Vora also notes we must realize that doing these things consistently is key because, "Trust is built one step at a time."

This begs the question: What steps do we take to build trust? Here are two challenge questions to kickstart thinking.

1. Can the people you work with, your friends, and your family trust you? Explain why.

2. What have you done (and what are you doing) to earn or expand that trust? Explain why.

Ponder these questions. Jot down some ideas. Then, consider the four benchmarks Greene and Howe put forth that measure trustworthiness. Here is what we must consider:

**Credibility** – Can people trust the words we speak based on our knowledge or credentials? This is the most fundamental (and least involved) level of trust.

**Reliability** – Do we do what we say we will do? Are we dependable to our team (or friends, family, etc.)?

**Intimacy** – Can people feel safe and secure with information they share with us? We would never violate a confidentiality or embarrass anyone. This is the highest level.

But these must be weighed against one's **self-orientation.** i.e., What is their primary focus? Is it on his or herself, or on others? For example, there could be someone we do not put much trust in because they seem to be overly concerned with how they appear. This is the inverse and must be factored. The overarching question we must ask ourselves is this:

 What is our level of self-orientation? i.e., Do we put our needs, feelings, and desires first? Or do we think of others first? Jot down some thoughts.

**Homework:** What do you think about these ideas. What are one or two things (action items) you can do this coming week to build trust with a friend, work team, or family?

**For additional reading:** Greene, C. & Howe, A. (2011). *The Trusted Advisor Fieldbook: A Comprehensive Toolkit for Leading with Trust.* http://trustedadvisor.com/why-trust-matters/understanding-trust/understanding-the-trust-equation

Vora, Tanmay (March 7, 2023). *Three Levels of Trust in Relationships.* Available at: https://qaspire.com/three-levels-of-trust-in-relationships/

## General Reflections:

One thing that struck me about this topic was: _____
_____

I'm still pondering *(and may seek more information on)*: _____
_____

As a result of this reflection, I plan to: _____
_____
_____

## Conversation 38

### The Power of Vision: An Indispensable Skill

**Purpose:** Have you ever thought about how you might bring the power of visioning to a small team or an organization to help them see the future (or the way to finish a project!)? Understanding how to summarize a concept and cast a vision of it can make you indispensable to your organization.

Consider this:

 Think of an example when you saw someone cast a vision of the future. (Not science fiction or our nation's economy, but a vision of a tangible program or initiative at your workplace.)

What did they do to get others on board?

How did they capture attention and help people see the potential?

**Background:** Teams, organizations, and even individuals often get stuck on a variety of things for a variety of reasons. One powerful mechanism that can un-stick a group is to help members see a vision of the future—where you're going and what is possible.

Leadership guru Andy Stanley says stating a vision is a way of describing a *preferred* future. It is a mental picture of *what could be.* But realize too that it's fueled by a *conviction* that it *should* be. People and organizations often do not pause long enough to summarize where a project is going by describing a clear, simple vision of that future state. Sometimes, they just need to be reminded to do it.

**The Discussion:** How might you bring the power of visioning to a small team or an organization to help them see the future? The short answer is to help them drill down to find their *why,* and then provide clarity of a future vision.

I have been many meetings where we're stymied by a myriad of details that may or may not be all that important. But during those meetings, when we (*if* we) pause and drill down to the *why,* there is a powerful, palpable energy shift, and we quickly devise our path forward. Focusing on mission (the why) can direct incremental action steps. But groups often need the reminder.

Here's a question to ponder:

>  Could you develop the skill of observing, clarifying, and describing a vision of the potential future? Remember, this can be done at an individual, team, or even organizational scale. Jot a few ideas on how that might look. How would you do this?

Most people have not studied how to do this. So don't worry. But it is not that complicated. Here's an approach anyone can use.

When stuck or stymied during a meeting, ask the group to press pause.

Then remind folks of *what could be* based on your main goal or mission. (This is the "why" you are even holding the meeting.) Remember, the *"could be"* should be fueled by a *conviction* of what *"should be."*

1. Summarize the big concepts. State them simply. Stanley says, "Memorable is portable." Keep it short. It's about what, not how. (You'll circle back to the *how*.)

2. Cast a vision convincingly. Summarize the problem and offer a solution (or prompt the group to change their perspective and imagine possibilities). The key is to explain why, drilling to the biggest *why* or main goal.

**Summary:** If you can help people (or a team or an organization) refocus on the mission, a vision can emerge that will direct the detail work (the needed action steps) because they will be tied to the higher purpose (the bigger *why*). This can be powerful for any group.

**Source:** Stanley, Andy (2016). *Making Vision Stick*. Leadercast 2016: Architects of Tomorrow. Available at: https://youtu.be/zAOg_rGVlr4

## General Reflections:

One thing that struck me about this topic was: _____
_____

I'm still pondering *(and may seek more information on)*: _____
_____

As a result of this reflection, I plan to: _____
_____
_____

**Conversation 39**

## Storytelling: A Useful Tool in Any Career

**Purpose:** To illustrate how telling stories can be a powerful means of helping you make connections, support your work, and advance organizational mission attainment.

**Background:** Early in my career, I spent a half-dozen years with a Fortune 500 company in the paper industry. There, I saw smart engineers and managers often giving one-way streams of information or direction to union workers, and I saw brilliant union workers attempting to share production information with management. Most often, I saw frustrated people on both sides because their conversations did not take the time to share the *why*. Telling a worker to do something differently without giving context is detrimental to your objective. Telling a manager that something you're trying is not working is okay, but they need to know *why*. That is critical. If we can include storytelling in the mix, communication in both directions becomes enhanced, and your objective stands a much greater chance of being achieved.

 If connection is critical to career success, think about how storytelling might enhance your opportunities. How might using stories help? Jot a few ideas here.

-
-
-

**The Discussion:** So how might stories help us in our work? This is a straightforward concept. When we tell stories in the traditional sense, we *create narrative* which is a social science construct. We focus on sense-making, morals, instruction, or perhaps an aesthetic. We weave concepts and subject material to engage in some way. The story helps our audience focus on the content, providing a place to begin inquiry. Ultimately, as they listen and begin to understand the context, they provide the *why*.

Return with me to the early 1990s and my paper industry days. There, I quickly learned that if we could include a quick story of *why* some change was needed, both union papermakers and engineer managers would quickly adopt the process and begin making progress. It just wasn't that complicated. But it took focus and deliberate attention to make it happen.

Stories are illustrative. They provide context and perspective, and they can make the abstract concrete. Stories can also move us (emotionally, and physically) to action.

Storytelling can be useful to anyone working to make positive change happen (or respond to events) in the workplace. But the approach also works at home. Please ponder these questions:

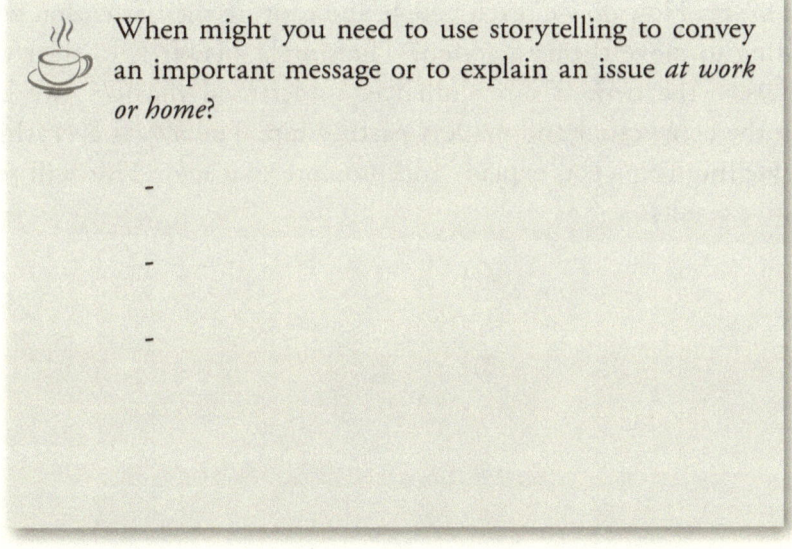

When might you need to use storytelling to convey an important message or to explain an issue *at work or home*?

-

-

-

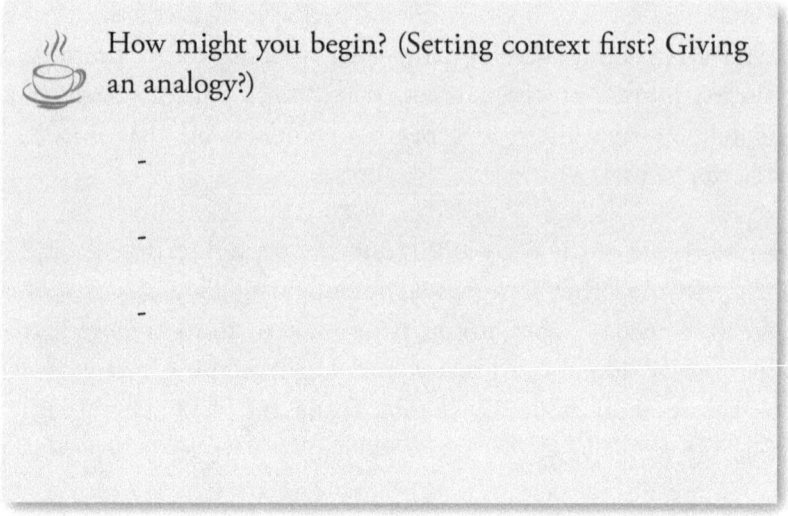

Storytelling can also provide you with the opportunity to see something from a different perspective. (See Conversations 34 and 35, as well as many others that challenge you to think about things from a different point of view.) A story can help your listener (or a group) make that shift so they can see the issue in a different way. This is a significant opportunity that is often missed.

**Summary:** How do we reach people and capture their attention when needing to move them to action? The simple answer is to start with context – the *why*. If our audiences understand the *why*, we have built the connection and made a partnership. The *why* is everything. Storytelling helps you explain and promote that *why*. This will yield positive results.

## General Reflections:

One thing that struck me about this topic was: _____
_____

I'm still pondering *(and may seek more information on)*: _____
_____

As a result of this reflection, I plan to: _____
_____
_____

**Conversation 40**

## Leading with Humility

**Purpose:** To remind us that potential is expanded when we lead with humility. Though this is the final of these forty conversations, it might just be the most important. Humility is a critical skill in leadership—leadership at all levels. Humble attitudes and approaches will encourage a positive organizational (or team or family) culture, and that *culture* will have a much greater impact on achieving your mission than any strategic plan of work. The good news is that humility can be cultivated and developed at both individual and organizational levels. Here's an initial question for consideration.

>  Can an attitude of humility help a leader (at any level) expand potential and achieve positive outcomes? Describe how you think a humble approach might help.

**Background:** It is reported that Frank Lloyd Wright defined an expert as "someone who has stopped thinking because he knows." We all know that person. Or maybe several. If they are leading a team, organization, volunteer project, or (this last one might be uncomfortable) your family, they could likely improve outcomes if they'd simply stop talking and invite others to provide input.

The painful question we all must ask ourselves is this: *How often do I think I'm the expert?* (Ouch.)

**The Discussion:** In 2013, Former MIT professor Edgar Schein published *Humble Inquiry.* Schein asked how an organization can get all the bosses (leaders) to create a climate where those under them feel free to engage. He said upward communication is often lacking in business, but leaders could make strides if they did three things:

1. Do less telling.
2. Learn to do more asking.
3. Do a better job of listening and acknowledging.

> Of the three items above, where are some places you might:
>
> 1. Do less telling. _____
>    _____
>
> 2. Learn to do more asking. _____
>    _____
>
> 3. Do a better job of listening and acknowledging.
>    _____

Schein claims that if we wish to find our own *original, individualized answers* (solutions to problems), then we will be required to do a deeper kind of search. In other words, our human *experience* is a necessary component of adult learning, knowledge synthesis, and the ultimate application. By inviting and listening to diverse inputs, we greatly expand potential to move toward our goals.

What does this mean for us today? In brief, when we face challenging questions, Schein suggests we "live with the question" for a bit. Sleep on it. Allow our imaginations and our brain power time to work while also inviting naïve questions and input. Those naïve questions can be the best kind because they look at the issue with a beginner's mind and ask about the fundamentals. Again, the experts are often too close to the subject to see what they're missing, or (as in Wright's quote) they quit thinking or asking because they believe they already have the answer. Even if you are not leading a team or project, using a humble inquiry approach can bring results in your personal life.

Questions to ponder:

 What is a current project where you might do less telling and more listening? (This could be at home or work.)

How might your team (or colleagues or family) respond? (Might they become more creative? Might they take more ownership? Might they grow personally or professionally by being permitted to try, even if they fail?) Jot some ideas.

**Summary:** What do you think about Schein's approach? Here are two more questions to ponder:

 How can you use *humble inquiry* to expand potential and positive outcomes?

Could inviting diverse input lead to the discovery of opportunity? (Describe an example for work, and one for a home or personal application.)

**Homework:** Think about approaching your own leadership with humility. During this upcoming week, look for an example of a time when you might have a choice to *inquire and listen*, or to *talk*. Give the first one (*inquire and listen*) a try. Take note of whether this was easy, or if it felt a bit uncomfortable. Try to focus on the *listening* part. Remember, every single person on the planet knows things you do not know. Imagine the increased potential if we learn from and with them.

## General Reflections:

One thing that struck me about this topic was: _____
_____

I'm still pondering *(and may seek more information on)*: _____
_____

As a result of this reflection, I plan to: _____
_____
_____

# 20 Bonus Questions to Encourage Continued Thinking

# 20 Bonus Questions to Encourage Continued Thinking

**Purpose:** To consider additional questions that will continue and deepen your thinking. These are for pondering anytime (with your mentor, a friend, or in your own brain).

**Background:** Great questions can powerfully move people to act, to get unstuck, and to see potential. These questions are conversation-starters that I have collected over many years. Some are similar, or they reinforce, concepts you've thought through in the forty conversations. But I have included some additional and nuanced questions to further challenge your thinking.

**Homework:** Use these perspective questions for additional personal and professional growth. Challenge yourself to do one per week. Start with a question that resonates. Consider how you might explore it further through reading or study. Prompt yourself to go deeper. Jot down your key thoughts. Then, talk with a mentor or friend about any questions that arise, or about any discoveries.

For your final challenge, after considering each question, pause to reflect on one aspect of gratitude you might find in your response. That is, jot down an appreciation you have, even if it's simply for the opportunity to keep learning. This will reinforce your gratitude practice which is something we all need to do. Opportunities abound. You're on a good journey.

## The Questions:

1. What is the world teaching you right now?

   _____

   _____

   _____

   I'm grateful for _____

   _____

2. When have you made an impact that you felt was significant?

   _____

   _____

   _____

   I'm grateful for _____

   _____

3. What would a close friend say your strengths are? (Do you agree?)

   _____

   _____

   _____

   I'm grateful for _____

   _____

4. How might you further develop your strengths?
   _____
   _____
   _____

   I'm grateful for _____
   _____

5. What does success look like for you? What can you do well that will help you get there?
   _____
   _____
   _____

   I'm grateful for _____
   _____

6. What obstacles are you facing?
   _____
   _____
   _____

   I'm grateful for _____
   _____

7. What are you not doing that might be keeping you from success?

   _____

   _____

   _____

   I'm grateful for _____

   _____

8. What can you control (versus what can you not control?) What options might you deploy?

   _____

   _____

   _____

   I'm grateful for _____

   _____

9. Think about a time when you felt like you failed. How did you bounce back? What did you actually do? (In the short-term, and over time?)

   _____

   _____

   _____

   I'm grateful for _____

   _____

10. Describe a recent setback. How are you recovering?

_____

_____

_____

I'm grateful for _____

_____

11. What leadership skills would you like to develop?

_____

_____

_____

I'm grateful for _____

_____

12. Who was the best teacher you ever had? Explain why.

_____

_____

_____

I'm grateful for _____

_____

13. Is there anything you pretend you understand, but you really don't? How might you gain understanding?

    _____

    _____

    _____

    I'm grateful for _____

    _____

14. When you were young, what did you *really* like doing? Can you capture the spirit or essence of that today in your work?

    _____

    _____

    _____

    I'm grateful for _____

    _____

15. If you were NOT here right now (in your job, etc.), what would you be doing? Like *right now*?

    _____

    _____

    _____

    I'm grateful for _____

    _____

16. If you could have really high skill in one area, what would it be? Why?

 I'm grateful for _____


17. If you could invite anyone living or dead to dinner, who would it be?

 I'm grateful for _____


18. What are you reading?

 I'm grateful for _____

19. Where do you need the most help? Where can you get help?

_____

_____

_____

I'm grateful for _____

_____

20. What topic have you not explored? What would you like to explore?

_____

_____

_____

I'm grateful for _____

_____

# In summary

I hope the question prompts in this journal have helped you to grow personally and professionally. I hope you will continue to reflect on these ideas (returning to this journal on occasion) as you move to create the future life you want and fulfill your personal mission. This kind of deep thinking and reflection can help you discover positive pathways in life and career trajectories with great possibility.

You're on your way. Press on with gratitude. Enjoy the journey.

## A Challenge:

Now that you have thought through some of the most important questions in life, consider this.

*How might you feel about mentoring someone else?*

You do not need formal training. You do not need a structured program. You do not need to spend time preparing for mentoring meetings. The only requirement to become an excellent mentor is your willingness to ask a few prompting questions, *and then to listen.*

That's it. Oh, and guess what? You can extract the prompting questions from this journal. You need not formalize anything. Just find a person or two, choose one of the forty conversation prompts, and casually enter a conversation.

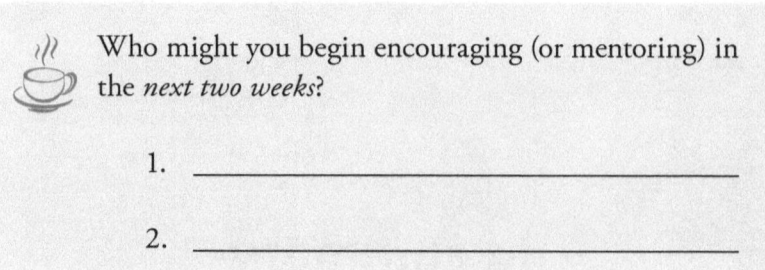

> Who might you begin encouraging (or mentoring) in the *next two weeks*?
>
> 1. _____
> 2. _____

The question prompts in this book can open very powerful and encouraging conversations. If you wish to learn more and be more deliberate in your mentoring (including learning the basics on how mentoring parallels adult learning theory, and behind-the-scenes context for doing great mentor work), you could read *The Encouraging Mentor: Your Guide to 40 Conversations that Matter*. This book includes these same prompting questions you've just completed, but with greatly expanded background, context, and some extra teaching and mentoring tips. It is available at http://encouragingmentor.com

*The Encouraging Mentor* book closes with this same challenge to go and encourage someone. *Encouragement* is what mentoring is all about. And as noted in the full-length book, encouragement has a dual impact. If you are feeling down or sad or tired or depressed, *go encourage someone*. Taking action will help *you* to feel better. It will lift your spirit as you lift theirs. Like love, the more encouragement you give away, the more you receive.

A longer-term challenge:

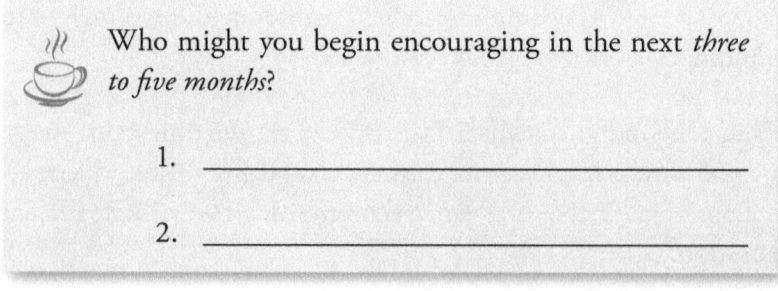

> Who might you begin encouraging in the next *three to five months*?
>
> 1. _____
> 2. _____

Did you write a name or two above? Again, do not feel like you need to study or take a seminar on mentoring. Just reach out and ask someone these simple, but deeply meaningful questions. You can positively change their lives.

## A final challenge:

As you reach out to mentor others, formally, informally, or non-formally, one of the best things you can do is to continue paying attention to your own personal and professional growth. My final challenge to you (I promise, this is the last one!) is to look back on the second part of Conversation 14, *"Listening to Yourself: 8 Dimensions of Wellness."* Review the eight areas and read over what you wrote. Then ask yourself one final reflective question:

Is there one dimension that stands out as foundational such that if you worked on solidifying it, many of the other dimensions would fall into place?

My foundational wellness dimension: _____
_____

Some of us might want to choose two foundational dimensions. That's okay. But please challenge yourself—and remind yourself—that if you can make progress here, other aspects of wellness can improve and solidify because you have a strong foundation.

As you build on that foundation, know that you will have times of struggle. Be open to that. Be open to change and growth. Along your journey, do not forget that you should never hesitate to reach out and ask for help when needed. We are made for community. Together, we can help each other recognize and reach our potential. In this process of personal growth, we will also help make our world a better place.

## Share Your Story

Dear Reader,

As you complete a portion—or all—of this journal, I would love to hear about your experience. For example, did one of the conversations catch your attention in a significant way? Did you have any ah-ha moments? Did you make a new determination, or were you inspired to change something in your personal or professional life?

You might also think about conversations that challenged you. Did one or two take a while to sink in? Was there one that simply didn't work for you? Each person will have a unique experience on the journey.

Personal and professional growth is, in a word, personal. But if you would like to share, I'd love to hear from you. My goal is to continuously improve my teaching. I want to share the best approaches and insights with my students (and my future readers). By sharing, you can help that process.

Please take a moment, go online, and share a brief comment, or a story: http://encouragingmentor.com

Thank you! And my best wishes on your continued journey.

## With Thanks:

I am thankful beyond measure for all the family, friends, pastors, teachers, coaches, mentors, coworkers, and even occasional strangers who encouraged me through the years.

I'm especially grateful to my family: Jill, my spouse of twenty-five years, and our daughters Abbey and Claire who have taught us more than we can imagine and brought us more joy than we knew was possible. The love, support, and encouragement of my immediate *and extended* family is beyond measure.

Lastly, I am thankful to *you* for reading and studying and applying some of the ideas in this book. I pray that they will help and encourage you in all aspects of life, and that you may share that encouragement with others.

# About the Author

Brian Raison's life mission is to encourage others. He has endeavored to practice this while serving at The Ohio State University for over twenty-five years. He teaches on campus and statewide helping students and Ohioans build capacity so they can improve their lives and livelihoods.

His teaching and research focus on leadership (coaching, mentoring, professional development), strategic alignment (at organizational scale), and work in understanding the power of diversity for mission attainment. He's passionate about improving connections to effect positive change.

As a professor, Brian serves as a Leadership Field Specialist with OSU Extension and teaches graduate courses in the Dept. of Agricultural Communication, Education, and Leadership. He holds a bachelor of science from OSU's Fisher College of Business, a master's in Sociology from Ohio University, Athens, and a PhD in Extension Education (non-formal andragogy and research) also from Ohio State.

Brian volunteers with his family in several faith-based service organizations across the U.S. and overseas. He carries on storytelling and heirloom gardening traditions learned from his grandparents.

# Also Available

## The Encouraging Mentor: Your Guide to 40 Conversations that Matter

*A how-to manual for managers, coaches, teachers, leaders, pastors, family, and friends who care.*

Copyright © 2024 by Brian Raison

This is a how-to book that offers step-by-step instructions to help you become a great mentor. It uses the same question prompts as in this *40 Conversations Journal*, but provides additional background and context to help you engage those you begin to mentor.

Brian has used these tools for nearly thirty-five years (in teaching university undergraduate, graduate, and adult audiences). He also uses them when helping teams and organizations think strategically about their future.

*The Encouraging Mentor* book can be used to start a mentoring program in your organization. It describes a nonformal mentoring approach—grounded in adult learning theory—that allows you to deploy tools at the right time to help people (or groups) grow when they are ready. This is a deliberate departure from standard *formal* mentoring programs that sometimes fail. This nonformal approach will equip your organization in helping people become more than they thought possible.

As an individual, this book will equip *you* to make a positive difference in someone's life.

Ordering information is available here: **http://encouragingmentor.com**

www.ingramcontent.com/pod-product-compliance
Lightning Source LLC
Chambersburg PA
CBHW020656220526
45464CB00001B/451